ATTAIN WISDOM TO CONQUER EVIL

THE
REAL
EXORCIST

RYUHO OKAWA

IRH PR

BOOKS

IRH PRESS
New York

ISBN 13: 978-1-942125-67-9
ISBN 10: 1-942125-67-4

Printed in Canada

First Edition

Contents

CHAPTER ONE

The Modern Exorcist

CHAPTER TWO

Basic Measures to Overcome Spiritual Disturbance

From Basic Knowledge to Practical Application

CHAPTER THREE

The Real Exorcist

The Power to Ultimately Win Against the Devil

6. **Through Faith, Become One with God**

CHAPTER FOUR

Exorcists as Religious Professionals

Q&A Session on "The Real Exorcist"

Q1 How to Check One's Faith

Translator's Note: This book is the English translation of two original Japanese books compiled together: *Gendai no Exorcist* (Chapter 1) and *Shin no Exorcist* (Chapters 2-4).

PREFACE

I have taken real stories from my own spiritual battles to compile this textbook. Almost every day, I am approached and confronted by evil spirits, devils, and *ikiryo* (the combination of the strong thoughts of a living person and that of his or her guardian spirit).

Essentially, the right approach is to teach the Truth to each spirit and send each one back to heaven. You must discern the primary cause of the spirit's suffering or the reason why the spirit is maliciously attacking living people. Then you must logically and rationally refute its argument, and clearly indicate which direction it should go in order to return to heaven. Unless the primary cause is eliminated, exorcism is impossible.

To achieve this end, you need to discipline yourself every day. Studying the Truth, undergoing spiritual discipline, having faith, and practicing altruism are indispensable. If you believe yourself to be someone special and become conceited, or if you are constantly swayed by greed, anger, and delusion, you will not be able to find salvation. The habit of humbly and diligently making efforts will also save you in the spiritual sense.

Ryuho Okawa
Master and CEO of Happy Science Group
April 5, 2019

TN: This preface was given for the Japanese title, *Shin no Exorcist* (compiled as chapters 2-4 of this book).

Note:

The nature of our mind is governed by "the Law of Same Wavelengths." If a person has negative thoughts, he or she will attract a hellish spirit with a similar mindset and be possessed by it. The phenomenon that occurs between the possessed person and the possessing spirit of hell is called "spiritual disturbance." In other words, spiritual disturbance is the harmful effect caused by a spirit. When a person is under negative spiritual influence, it means he or she is possessed by an evil spirit.

When you suffer spiritual disturbance, you will often feel ill or become sick. You will start to have all sorts of complaints and voice your dissatisfaction, causing negative influences on your relationships and work performance, and it will eventually lead your life to ruin. To overcome spiritual disturbance, you need to reflect on your thoughts and deeds and correct any mistakes, have a well-balanced lifestyle, and turn your mind to the heavenly world. These practices will allow you to be free of negative spiritual influences.

Chapter One

The Modern Exorcist

Lecture given on June 23, 2001
at General Headquarters, Happy Science, Tokyo, Japan

What are Devils?

The notion of devils is familiar in Western society

This chapter deals with a slightly unusual topic, "The Modern Exorcist." You may know the term "exorcist" because some decades ago there were movies with this word in their titles. Even if you are not familiar with these films, you have probably heard of the term one way or another.

An exorcist is someone who exorcises devils. The notion of a devil is very familiar to those raised in the Christian culture; everyone knows what devils are and many Christians actually believe in their existence. In Japan, however, people have limited knowledge about devils, and many seem to imagine them only as creatures that appear in fairy tales or folktales.

Japanese people may be more familiar with the term *oni* (ogre). Since ancient times, ogres have appeared in Japanese stories. But what has been referred to as *oni* is actually a devil, or demon. Devils are in fact what the Japanese call *oni*.

In the movie *The Exorcist*, the terms "demon" and "devil" were used differently depending on the context.

The word "demon" was used for an evil spirit or malicious spirit, and "devil" for a more powerful creature with a horrible face and horns on its head, like those often depicted on playing cards. The movie used these words differently in this way.

Thus, devils are very familiar to Westerners, while Japanese people only have a vague idea of them. Perhaps Japanese people associate the image of a devil with Christianity.

Devils appear in different religions

This being said, devils appear in Buddhist scriptures as well. In India, there are devils called Namuci and Mara-Papiyas. Mara is the Sanskrit word for devil. When it was translated into Chinese, the written Chinese word for devil was formed for the first time by combining two characters, the character for hemp for the sound and the one for demon for the meaning. The existence of devils is also widely accepted in India.

In Christian religions, Lucifel is the most powerful devil. He used to be one of the seven archangels and is commonly known as Lucifer. He now has the strongest power in hell. There is also a devil named Beelzebub that tried constantly to tempt Jesus while he fasted and wandered the desert for forty days. This devil said to

Jesus, "If you will fall down and worship me, I will give you all the kingdoms of the world." The devil also tempted Jesus by saying, "If you are the Son of God, command that these stones become bread." Jesus rebuked him, saying, "It is written [in the Old Testament], 'You shall not tempt the Lord, your God.'" Beelzebub is another very strong devil.

It has been more than twenty years since I attained Great Enlightenment (at the time of this lecture). If I am to reveal the number of times I have been confronted by Lucifel and Beelzebub during this time, it has been a few hundred times for Lucifel and much less for Beelzebub— perhaps ten. On the other hand, devils from the Indian tradition, such as Mara-Papiyas or Namuci, have never appeared before me. Perhaps they still remain in the Indian domain and have yet to come to Japan.

As for the Buddhism-related devils, Kakuban appears before me the most. In the spiritual messages that I published during the early times of Happy Science (now compiled into *A Collection of Spiritual Messages by Ryuho Okawa* [published by Happy Science]), there are some descriptions of this devil, but I used asterisks in place of his name to avoid any trouble arising.

Kakuban is a devil associated with esoteric Buddhism. There are many temples of this sect in Japan. If I were to list their names at the risk of giving rise to problems, the famous Hase Temple in Nara Prefecture and a temple in

Otowa, Bunkyo Ward in Tokyo, for example, worship him. Kakuban started Shingi Shingon (the Reformed Shingon school), a faction of esoteric Buddhism that derived from the Shingon sect, and he was said to have revived the Shingon sect. He was later given the posthumous title of Kogyo-Daishi, and in this sense, he is now more or less respected. But while alive, he was actually persecuted by orthodox groups of the Shingon sect for having given highly heretical, misguided teachings. He was forced to flee to the mountains of Negoro to continue his activity as a monk of esoteric Buddhism. Once persecuted, a person tends to be treated as a hero, and in the same way, he earned respect after death.

The reason Kakuban was persecuted was that his teachings were misguided. Despite this, many temples that follow his school of thought were built, and there are people who still believe in his teachings. That is why I deliberately avoided mentioning his name in the early days, and instead used asterisks. This devil is the one from the Buddhist domain that bothers me most often.

Kakuban is involved in two of the new Japanese religious groups today, deluding followers in many ways. One is an esoteric Buddhist group based in Kyoto, and another is a new religious group based in Tokyo that focuses on spiritual powers. Kakuban entered these groups when they were being established and continues to misguide them.

Esoteric Buddhism, in particular, needs to be cautious of this devil, because its teachings are closely associated with spiritual power. If followers start to worship spiritual power, this devil will come in and delude them. Since esoteric Buddhism strongly emphasizes spiritual power, followers need to make sure they are connected to the right spirits; otherwise, various evil beings will approach them from the other world.

In esoteric Buddhism, there is a frightening sect called the Tachikawa-ryu school, which worships painted skulls. This religion is not of Japanese origin but has its roots in Tibet.

In 1995, a new Japanese religious group based on Tibetan esoteric Buddhism caused a series of tragic incidents that killed many people in Japan. This religion claimed its authenticity, insisting that its roots lie in Tibetan esoteric Buddhism. The truth, however, is that the devil had already entered Tibetan esoteric Buddhism itself, the very source. When I read the writings of the Tibetan esoteric Buddhist leader called "Holy Master," I can clearly see that he is completely under the devil's influence.

In religious groups that focus on spiritual power, there is almost no one who can verify whether they are connected to a good or evil source, so they are not even aware if devils are involved. If their followers experience some spiritual phenomena, these religions can appear to be righteous groups. This is very frightening.

Thus, devils related to Christianity and esoteric Buddhism often appear before me. Devils related to Japanese Shinto also exist, but they have not often made an appearance. Perhaps Happy Science teachings are too difficult for them to understand, or they are too busy trying to influence the many sects that exist in Shintoism.

To cite an example, there is a powerful devil that has influence over a Shinto sect in Chiba Prefecture. This sect branched off from a Japanese religious group called Seicho-no-Ie, which teaches Light-Only Thinking. This thinking can serve to greatly inflame people's desires, depending on how it is interpreted. If it is taken to mean that one should just let his or her desires grow without any practice of self-reflection, and only this aspect is emphasized, it will produce unrepentant people. As a result, devils will easily find their way into such groups and become active. This Shinto sect emphasizes the teaching that all bad events that happen in this world are signs of evil dissolving, but if this were true, people would have no need to self-reflect, repent, or correct their mistakes. Thus, devils are involved in such groups in the Japanese Shinto domain.

Following the same logic, devils are also active in certain Buddhist groups that rely only on divine salvation.

This does not mean that the founders of these schools of thought, such as Honen or Shinran, were manipulated by devils. They founded sects that rely only on divine salvation based on their acute, real experiences, but over the passage of time, devils found their way in.

An easy and indulgent path is truly dangerous. Once you follow a way of thinking that allows you to be quickly and easily forgiven whatever you do, devils will silently enter your mind. This is a harsh reality.

Distance yourself from an organization Influenced by evil spirits

There are an uncountable number of religious groups in the world, but many of the new religious groups today in particular are misguided and have bad reputations. They may not have been evil when they were founded, but once various spirits start to freely come down to them, devils come to replace them in time. When an organization grows to a certain size and gains influence and power, devils enter it to delude people.

If the leader of an organization has strong desires, he or she can neither stop the devil's interference nor perceive it. Many followers of such groups also have strong desires. When people who only seek worldly self-realization flock to an organization that focuses on teaching how to achieve one's worldly desires, they are unable to perceive evil influences in each other. This is how devils become involved in various religious organizations around the world.

The number of such religious groups is limitless. Although the total number of powerful devils is small, their minions and accomplices continually work to attract more evil spirits to form a huge group. So, in principle, it is better to keep your distance from such religious groups. It is best to concentrate on strengthening our own light and spreading the teachings of Happy Science, instead of trying to correct these groups' mistakes. Because there are just so many of them, if you try earnestly to correct their mistakes, you could end up falling prey to a devil, as in the saying, "Many go out for wool and come home shorn." This can sometimes happen, so it is very difficult.

The Origin of Evil Spirits and Devils

When lost spirits repeatedly do evil,
They become evil spirits

Many evil spirits retain a strong human nature. Spirits that cannot swiftly return to heaven after death are called "lost spirits." When these lost spirits have remained on earth for a certain period of time and start to cause harm to living people, we can call them "evil spirits." When negative spiritual phenomena occur to a family or to those who have some connection to a particular place or region, they are usually the workings of evil spirits.

There are office buildings with specific windows from which many people are said to have jumped to their death. At such places, there are earth-bound spirits; they remain in these places and try to drag other people down. There are coastal areas also well-known for suicides, and earth-bound spirits can be found in such places as well.

As lost spirits repeatedly commit evil, they gradually become evil spirits. The shorter the time a spirit wanders after death, the higher the possibility there is for it to be persuaded to return to heaven. But as the wandering period gets longer, it becomes harder for it to return to heaven. If the spirit has continued to harm living people for a long period of time, a short, teary self-reflection is not enough for it to be forgiven of its wrongdoings.

If I were to point out one problem with religions that rely only on divine salvation, it would be that they teach quick and easy salvation, when in fact sins are not forgiven so easily. Spirits that have repeatedly committed wrongdoings for hundreds or thousands of years have accumulated a great amount of sin. So even if they experience a change of heart after being admonished, there is the matter of how to clear up their accumulated past sins.

Not only have the spirits created darkness in their own minds, but they have also received negative thoughts of resentment from various people. Having become evil spirits, they dragged other people down to hell one after another, or caused spiritual disturbances to increase the number of their accomplices. Since these victims retain feelings of resentment toward them, the simple practice of self-reflection will not be enough for them to be forgiven. To a certain extent, they have to atone proportionately for the sins they have committed to clear them up.

For this reason, it is impossible to persuade devils back to heaven. They have spent too much time in hell. There are devils who have been in hell for one, two, or three thousand years, so it is almost impossible for them to return to heaven.

In fact, it is not that they cannot return to heaven; they have rather given up on returning to heaven. They form their base in hell and intend to make their lives easier there. Figuratively speaking, they are like gangs in this world going against police authorities. They are creating their own base and committing wrongdoings with others who share a similar mindset.

Some beings have accumulated so much evil that if they were to get out of the group and renounce their wrongdoings, they would feel like they were losing their identities. When this type of spirit possesses someone, it is impossible to persuade it to return to heaven, so it is better to not engage in conversation. It is best to just expel it. Otherwise there will be no end to your efforts, since the spirit cannot be saved through persuasion. It has committed too many evil deeds.

People in leadership positions Can easily become devils

Now, what type of person turns into a devil? An ordinary person can become an evil spirit if that person had evil thoughts or committed evil deeds. Those evil deeds do not have to be crimes; a person can become an evil spirit if he or she has lived with bad or dark thoughts. Evil spirits are those who had wicked hearts, always scheming, constantly arguing with others, deceiving or hurting other people, always raging, having no qualms about doing evil, and mainly living with destructive thought energy or emotions. Since they caused so much trouble to the people around them and made them suffer, they find themselves unable to return to heaven after death. They writhe in agony and become aggressive in a place called hell. This is the true nature of evil spirits.

Devils, however, have more influence and leadership, and use manipulation. People in leadership positions are the main source of those who become devils. For example, misguided political leaders or dictators can very easily become devils. Pol Pot, the Cambodian dictator who led the massacre of two million people, is undoubtedly a devil, and so are Hitler and Stalin. Those who mainly killed in political leadership positions become devils after death.

Of course, in times of war, heroic leaders may sometimes kill others, but the question is whether their actions were supported by justice or the great cause of God or Buddha. It also depends on the extent of the killing.

Angels of light often try to avoid killing people, despite being in positions that would enable them to do so. Take, for example, Kaishu Katsu [1823–1899], a prominent samurai during the Meiji Restoration. Despite being an expert in sword fighting, he never killed a man.

Kogoro Katsura [1833–1877], later known as Takayoshi Kido, was also a sword master, but he never killed a man either. Whenever there was risk of conflict, he would always flee to avoid it. It was very rare for a samurai of that era to have not killed a single person. Angels of light do not like killing by nature, so they often flee to avoid confrontation.

This being said, sometimes it cannot be helped when political or military leaders have no choice but to take the lives of others to achieve a truly lofty ideal. There are times when action must be taken to bring down an evil regime or change an old era. In these cases, such actions are permitted. Otherwise, leaders are apt to become devils if they have killed a large number of people because of their deep-rooted taste for cruelty or brutality, or by exercising their power and ruling over others using fear.

In addition to political and military leaders, ideological leaders who have deluded or brainwashed many people with misguided ideas also become devils. Those who are likely to become devils are people who had a great influence on many others and ended up creating great evil.

There are also differences in the power of devils. In modern society, some journalists and members of the press have a great influence in the world. Those who strive only to fulfill their own desires instead of serving society or achieving justice will become demons, low-level devils with five or six minions. There are many who turn out like this.

There are others who become like this among philosophers and authors whose work is to express their ideas. A novelist could become a leading demon by writing many evil novels to mislead or delude a lot of people. Hellish literature is quite popular in this world, and even famous writers could become devils after death. Those who have had a great influence on people to corrupt them and ruin their lives actually have a natural disposition to become devils. The same is true for government officials who live only for their desire for power and do not have compassion in their hearts.

Religious leaders also have a great influence on a large number of people, so leaders of misguided religious groups will certainly become devils and will have almost no hope of returning to heaven. They have not only given wrong teachings but have also misled the lives of many people. What is worse, not only did they deceive people on earth, they have also dragged them to hell, forming a base with their followers in the other world. They, too, are devils, embodiments of evil.

Deluding people's minds is a serious sin. There are so many of these devils that almost nothing can be done, but there is no point complaining about this. I look over the world like a globe, imagining lights flicking on one after another in different places, just like a city gradually lights up at night. The world does not become suddenly bright because there is pitch-black all around, but I am trying to light up the world little by little. Since we cannot forcibly change other people's hearts, we would rather focus our energy on what we can do.

Desires open the way to becoming a devil

Humans are indeed weak; the primary reason for people to become devils lies in the desires they have. Desires are where devils make their home. However, as long as we live in physical bodies, we cannot completely extinguish these desires. Desires are part of our power to live, so it is not possible to eliminate them altogether. For this reason, devils will never cease their existence. Since there are always sources of supply, new devils are constantly born. Human desires are their foothold, the foundation of their lives.

There is certainly some degree of justness in desires. Everyone seeks freedom and wants to achieve their goals. They want to be important, control others, and criticize the faults of others while shutting their eyes to their own shortcomings. This is human nature. In a way, it represents human weakness or cowardliness, the least respectful aspect of human beings. We could call it mediocrity. Since this is the foothold of devils, devils will not completely cease to exist.

Desires cannot be completely eliminated. That is why I teach how to control desire, like controlling the flow of traffic. At intersections, traffic is regulated by traffic lights or police officers' hand signals, but it is not possible to prevent the very desire or a person's wish to drive a car. Cars are meant for driving, and we cannot just stop wanting to drive. There are so many people wanting to drive cars that roads are packed with them.

We want to drive, and so do others; but if everyone drove as freely as they please, accidents would occur. In fact, these accidents are the evil part. Because so many people in this world are living at the mercy of their desires, they crash into others, causing evil to arise.

What, then, is necessary to eliminate this evil? If people decided to abandon owning or driving cars, there would certainly be no collisions. But this would also result in hindering people's freedom and self-realization. That is why cars will not be abolished.

In Japan, some automakers have made profits of over ¥1 trillion (about US$10 billion), despite the fact that seven thousand people die every year in car accidents (at the time of the lecture). This is hard to believe, but it shows that human desires are much stronger, or that people find greater merit in driving. It means people feel grateful for being able to drive cars even if about seven thousand fatalities are caused by traffic accidents. This is understandable because it would be extremely inconvenient and time-consuming to walk, for example, from Tokyo to Osaka like in the olden days.

I plan to write a biography of Shakyamuni Buddha, but it will not be so easy because he spent much time walking. Almost all year long, he would travel the bumpy roads of India, so there is not much to write about. The distance between the Jetavana and Venuvana monasteries is roughly the same as the distance between Tokyo and Osaka. But every year Shakyamuni Buddha went back and forth between these monasteries on foot. Following his example, many Buddhists now train themselves in the practice of mountain walking. For Shakyamuni Buddha however, since there was no modern means of transportation in olden times, he had no choice but to walk the distance.

Shakyamuni Buddha would spend hundreds of days a year walking, and the only time he did not walk was during the rainy season. During the rainy season, he would spend about three months at one location and practice meditation. In this way, he spent almost all his life either walking or meditating in a single location, so there was not much drama in his life.

Returning to my point, in today's society, the very act of removing the desire to drive cars could be considered evil. If someone told people that they should go back to riding horses, going by palanquin, or going by foot over long distances instead of riding in a car, this might be considered an act of evil. So, cars will not cease to exist. But this means that accidents will occur, giving rise to new evil. This is the current situation.

Human desires include the desire to be happy. This desire itself cannot be denied, so it is important to regulate traffic skillfully and have everyone abide by the rules and drive during the course of one's life without causing any accidents. While it is fine for everyone to seek happiness, this effort should not lead to the misfortune of many others.

Then how can this be achieved?

That is the role of religion. The work of religion is to help many people live happily, preventing them from becoming miserable and committing mistakes. It is also to prevent people from going to hell and becoming devils after death, and from deluding people on earth as devils. That is why religions are active in many places around the world.

However, not all religious groups are righteous ones; there are also many misguided religions. When religion in general has a bad reputation in society, it is often the case that mistaken religions outnumber the righteous ones. Although there is a great need for religious work, it is difficult for people to ascertain whether a religion has ultimately produced good results. Since they cannot see the ultimate consequences in the other world, in many cases they cannot judge whether a certain religious group has truly benefited the people. This is an extremely difficult point.

Evil spirits and devils exist as an extension of human nature. While it is good for people to love themselves, those who loved themselves in mistaken ways have become evil spirits and devils. They resorted to victimizing other people as a result of the mistaken love for themselves. They believed that their happiness could only be achieved at the cost of others' happiness, that they could not be happy unless they caused trouble for others, gave them pain or worry, killed or hurt them, or made them fail. They had such views of life and selfishly struggled to attain happiness themselves, and eventually ended up becoming evil spirits or devils. This is the origin of evil spirits and devils.

Religious Value Systems are The Exact Opposite of Those of Devils

Religion purposely teaches Giving love and egolessness

Religion puts effort into teaching value systems that are exactly the opposite of those of devils. It teaches, "Love should not only mean love of oneself. It is important to give love. The act of giving love to others is essential. People mostly consider that love is to take, and only think about how to take love from others or be loved by others, and hardly ever about giving love to others."

Everyone wants to be loved. Both angels and devils have this feeling. However, angels have a strong tendency for self-sacrifice. They were people who fought for others, who willingly gave their lives for the sake of others. In this way, angels have a detached attitude to life. Devils, on the other hand, do not have such a graceful attitude. They have a desire to take everything from others and feel no remorse about it. For example, they do not think it is wrong to take love from others, deprive others of their beloved things and make them suffer, enslave others, force them to labor, and kill them if they disobey; they rather consider these as good deeds.

There is only a very subtle difference between giving love and taking love, and religion teaches this difference. It is certainly important that you value yourself and try to be happy, but most people do not think of anything else. If left as they are, such feelings only inflate. That is why I give the teaching of giving love and the Buddhist teaching of egolessness, to help people have a complete change of heart.

In Western society, it is considered important for humans to establish their egos, and that life without a sense of ego is seen as not worth living. People thus value life based on their egos. On the other hand, Buddhism teaches egolessness. From a Western perspective, not having an ego would mean losing your dignity as a human being. Western thinking holds that human rights and the right to seek happiness were born from the high regard for people's egos. Democracy is also for people to pursue their own happiness. This idea is basically right, so why, despite all that, did Shakyamuni Buddha give the teaching of egolessness?

It is difficult to become egoless. It is rare to see someone who endeavors to erase his or her ego when most people have a self-centered way of thinking; such a person may even seem insane by this world's standards. Even animals and plants are only concerned about self-preservation. In this environment of self-preservation, however, there will be people who are not really concerned about themselves. You can imagine Gandhi of India, for example. But strangely enough, these people who have abandoned their egos actually accomplish great work. The very existence of such people, who have disciplined themselves to eliminate their egos, can actually help save others who are living in accordance to their egos and creating suffering.

Everyone wants to be happy and is striving to boost their egos. But as people's egos clash, they start to hate one another, and even wage wars and start killing each other. They clash against each other and suffer as a result of boosting their egos and expanding their power and rights. If, at such times, an egoless person appears, these people who had worked hard to sharpen their egos begin to retract their pointed egos.

The horns on the devil's head are, in fact, the horns of its ego. These horns grow out when people are only concerned about themselves and become conceited. They gore others with their horns and make them suffer. This horn of ego is a heart that only thinks about fulfilling selfish desires such as desires for fame and status. If left as they are, humans will become like this; that is why religion must teach people to strive for an egoless state of mind and to give love to others.

Humans take the love of others instinctively. As long as we live in this world, we cannot completely do away with this tendency. It is impossible to live without taking other people's love. Even Mother Teresa took love from others; it was not possible for her to carry out her activities without taking other people's love. She was able to work because she received donations and help from government authorities and many people. Therefore, even if you have an egoless mind and give love to others, the truth is that you cannot live without receiving love from others. It is essential that your central thoughts are directed at giving, rather than taking.

The spirit of crucifixion is the same as The philosophy of egolessness

In Christianity, if Jesus was simply regarded as someone who failed in his missionary work and was ultimately crucified on the cross, his life would be seen as tragic, but Christians do not interpret his life in this way. In a sense, the Christian philosophy of crucifixion is close to Shakyamuni Buddha's philosophy of egolessness.

The son of God appeared on earth to save people, spoke truthfully from his heart and spoke passionately of God's Will without compromise. As a result, he was put to death on a cross. This was the life of Jesus. Through his life, he wanted to teach that there was truth that must be upheld even at the cost of his physical life. If he had lied and made a compromise, he could have avoided death. But if he had clung to his physical life, it would mean that he was the same as any other person in this world.

Jesus rode into Jerusalem on a donkey, knowing that he would eventually be crucified. Since he knew his fate, he should not have entered the city in the first place, but he intentionally gave his life away to fulfill what had been prophesied.

Some may say that Jesus still had some attachment to earthly life when he was praying in the Garden of Gethsemane and sweating drops of blood. It is written in the Bible that he prayed, "If it be possible, let this cup pass from me," and he sweat drops of blood that fell to the ground. But he finally made up his mind to accept his death, saying, "My Father, if this cup cannot pass unless I drink it, Your will be done."

Socrates had the same resolve when he chose to die by drinking a cup of poison. When Socrates was arrested and jailed, those around him tried hard to persuade him to escape his death sentence. Even the prison guard tried to let him flee, but Socrates' convictions did not change, and he chose to die for his beliefs. For him, escaping would have meant admitting his philosophy was a lie. Therefore, Socrates died for the sake of his own philosophy. On this point, he was similar to Jesus, and the two are now considered saints.

Some Gospels in the Bible state that Jesus cried out on the cross, "My God, my God, why have you forsaken me?" But this cannot be true; it would mean that Jesus was not enlightened, which is wrong.

It would almost be the same as claiming that Shakyamuni Buddha taught materialism. Shakyamuni Buddha taught the impermanence of all things, saying that the physical body is transient, that it will waste away and disappear, like floods wash a mud house away. Some scholars misinterpret this teaching to conclude that the Buddha was a materialist and did not believe in the soul. Such an interpretation of egolessness and the denial of the soul are wrong, and a similar mistake can be found in Christianity as well.

It was incorrect to interpret that Jesus cried out, "My God, my God, why have you forsaken me?" This is definitely not true. If it were true, Jesus' teachings would all be lies. While he was alive, Jesus would talk with spirits from the heavenly world, like I do now, so it could not be true. Jesus was actually calling out to the angels Elijah and Rafael, "The time has come for me to leave this world. Come take me away."

There were fools who misinterpreted Jesus' words as calling out for help and put such misinterpretation in the

Bible. One would not want to be such a shameful disciple. This description cannot be retracted from the Bible now. It is impossible to change a passage that has lasted for nearly two thousand years. If someone attempted to delete it, that person would be labeled a devil.

Such an interpretation was just the imagination of those who were not spiritually sensitive, who did not have the ability to talk with the spirits in the other world. Jesus was in no way a weak person. Shusaku Endo, for example, was a modern Japanese author who wrote about the life of Jesus. But his description of Jesus was so weak that his writing cannot bear reading. Writers tend to describe their main characters as similar to themselves, and Endo described Jesus as a projection of what he would do if he were Jesus. That is why his depiction of Jesus was that of such a weak man, and this is quite pitiful.

Spiritual leaders like Jesus always receive answers to their prayers. Ordinary people may not receive responses to their prayers, but Jesus did, and he actually conversed with spirits. As Jesus was praying in the Garden of Gethsemane, a spiritual being appeared and told him that he would die. That is why Jesus was prepared to die.

This spirit of crucifixion is the same as Shakyamuni Buddha's philosophy of egolessness. Jesus wanted to teach that although humans are attached to their physical bodies, they have eternal life that extends beyond their physical lives. He also wanted to teach that "God's Laws are not bound by Torah, Roman laws, or principles governed by the politics of this world. Even if obedience is enforced by military might, or weapons are used to achieve ambitions, God's Laws are unchangeable. Even if the temple of the body perishes, you can never destroy eternal life nor destroy God's words." Jesus was crucified to prove this truth.

Moreover, Jesus even resurrected after his crucifixion. He presented himself resurrected before many people so that his death would not be misinterpreted as the mere destruction of his physical body and the failure of his work in this world. According to the Bible, about five hundred people witnessed his resurrection. This number is large enough that it can only be considered a true occurrence. Without the resurrection, Christianity most probably would not have been established. This shows how hard it is for a true philosophy to be accepted.

The teachings of impermanence and egolessness Are an antithesis to devils

Looking at how Jesus died, it is obvious that Jesus' way of thinking was the direct opposite of the value systems of devils. Devils claim that this world will go on eternally, as seen in the way that Beelzebub tried to entice Jesus. They tempt people by trying to deceive them into thinking that the power, glory, and prosperity of this world will continue forever.

Buddha's teachings of the impermanence of all things and the egolessness of all phenomena may sound quite somber, but these are very important ideas in protecting oneself against devils. "All things are impermanent; there is nothing in this world that lasts forever or that can be preserved eternally. Everything is bound to perish. This body, or even a king, an emperor, a minister of state, or the glory of a family such as the Fujiwara Clan or the Taira Clan—everything will be gone. There is nothing in this world that is permanent. What is permanent, what is eternal, can only be found in the other world." This philosophy is a strong antithesis to devils.

Those who have devoted themselves to the teachings of God or Buddha and sincerely followed them to the end of their lives will join eternal brilliance and gain eternal lives. But those who have compromised themselves in this world and have lived for worldly luxury, glory, power, and money will perish despite their efforts to obtain eternal life. They will be cut down just like wheat in the harvest season. This is how it will appear.

This contrast of value systems shows the difference between people who have spiritual views on the world and feel the presence of God or Buddha close by and people who do not. For those who base their thinking on this world, stories of the spirit world and Buddha or God may sound like abstract philosophy or literature, no matter how many times they hear them. Some will be skeptical and feel that they might be being deceived. If their sense of values were turned around 180 degrees, everything would be clear, but even modern religious leaders and Christians fail to understand this.

4

Fight Against Devils
With Reason and Wisdom

Devils target people's desires

Devils always tempt people through their desires. Those undergoing religious discipline are not usually bad people; they do not lead evil lives and would not normally be possessed or controlled by devils. However, if they happen to be undergoing spiritual training near pivotal positions of spreading the Truth, such as working closely to Jesus or Buddha, even a slight wavering of their minds is targeted. While devils do not usually target ordinary people, they attack those at core positions of missionary work when they have the slightest wavering or desire in their hearts.

One of the easiest targets of devils is sexual desire. People cannot be completely free of this desire as long as they live a human life. It is said that sensual desire is the entrance and exit of spiritual discipline, and this is where devils set their target. Many practitioners of religious training are stoical, so devils find it even more enjoyable to tempt such people by inciting their desires. Ordinary people are not so stoical, so there is no point in devils tempting them. Even if they do, there would not be much effect; it would only slightly accelerate the people's desire, creating just a bit more confusion. So, they would rather pick on those who practice sexual abstinence to try to overturn their lives. Sexual desire is always being targeted.

The next target is the desire for food. But in countries where food is plentiful, devils would be unable to tempt people in the same way that a devil tempted Jesus with bread while fasting. Shakyamuni Buddha was also the target of the devil's attack while he was fasting before attaining enlightenment; he was tempted with food when he was hungry. In modern society, though, tempting with food is less common.

Another target is the desire for power or fame. Just like sexual desire, this is also an area that religious practitioners cannot escape. Religious practitioners especially have a strong desire for fame, and their desire for power also grows as their organization gets bigger. This is a very difficult battle, so how you deal with the desire for fame and power is important. "Can I always remember the original aspiration I had when I started my spiritual discipline? Can I return to the starting point, to my original intention? Can I see myself as just an ordinary practitioner of the Truth? Can I remain humble?" These are questions you need to consider.

You need obedience and humility to prevent devils from creeping into your desire for fame and power and agitating your mind. Obedience here means obedience to God or Buddha, to what is true, and to the teachings. This obedience and humility will protect you from devils. When your desire for fame gets stronger, it becomes harder to protect yourself.

In addition, intelligent people tend to have strong doubts. So, they pick on trifling matters to cause a stir. Thus, religious practitioners become targets through sexual desire, or their desire for fame and power.

Weaker problem-solving abilities create worries, Which devils use to find their way in

When we live on earth as humans, we cannot completely separate ourselves from worries and troubles associated with work, family, and other relationships. From ancient times, religious practitioners would often remain single because of the lesser burden on single people. A single person's living requirements are fewer, and it is easier to support oneself; there are fewer worries about family and less burden at work. All one has to worry about is feeding oneself, so it is a very simple way of life. This is why religious practitioners often stay single.

I believe it is good that there is a certain proportion of single religious practitioners in the world. In this way, there can be a balance in the world. The true form of a religious practitioner is to stay single and devote oneself solely to spiritual discipline. Undergoing religious training while supporting one's family entails a heavier burden; in terms of ability, it will require more than twice as much as an average salaried person.

A person who has a pure heart but fails in life usually has a low problem-solving ability. Problem-solving abilities are correlated to worldly work skills and wisdom. If one is lacking in these abilities, he or she cannot solve problems and will end up becoming overwhelmed by them. When this happens, no matter how pure his or her mind is, the person will move about in confusion and suffer sleepless nights.

Over the last twenty years, I have seen many people who, despite living with pure hearts, have ended up becoming victims of devils. The reason for their downturn was, in most cases, their lack of abilities at work. If one is overwhelmed by a problem that just cannot be solved, a devil will enter his or her wavering heart, and it cannot be repelled. Even if that person is not necessarily an evil person, he or she becomes a victim unless the root problem is solved. For example, when you cannot overcome a serious problem at work or you cannot find a solution to a trouble in your family no matter how much you try, you cannot be free of this worry and you will become obsessed by the problem. If, at such times, you are targeted by a devil, it is difficult to find an escape.

It is only natural that people have work or family concerns. But unless they have a sufficient problem-solving ability, or the ability to put an end to worries and rationally protect themselves, devils will delude them through worry, largely amplifying the trifling problem at work or in the family. It will create great confusion, and as a result, they will become devils' servants or slaves without realizing it. So, you have to think about how to overcome this situation.

Worldly abilities include the abilities you are born with and the ones you develop and acquire as you grow up, and these abilities vary between individuals. By nature, people have different dispositions, personalities, and degrees of intelligence; some are methodical while others are careless; some are tenacious and can engage in long-term work while others are impatient and can only accomplish short-term work.

What is needed when you do not have the aptitude for your current work or lack the abilities to accomplish it? If you are unable to overcome your problem and make your way through difficulties, the only way to solve your problem is to take a step back and withdraw. It is important to plan a strategic retreat. If you do not retreat, you will allow devils to enter your mind and create great confusion. When this happens, you will have no way to stop it.

If you find that your desire is excessive and your work is beyond your capacity, you could ask someone with more aptitude to take over the job. Or, if the work is too difficult for anyone to accomplish, you could reassess the goals to make them more realistic or ask advice from relevant people. You could consider, for example, extending the deadline, setting a longer timeline, setting a lower goal, or dividing the work into smaller parts to tackle them one at a time. In this way, you need to take a step back and break down the problem into smaller parts so it can fit into the range of your capabilities.

Even when you are presented with a feast, there is a limit to the amount of food you can put in your mouth. No matter how hard you may try, you cannot swallow a cow or a whole chicken in one bite. You can only eat a mouthful of food at a time. In the same way, there is a limit to how much work you can take on. You may think of good ideas and be passionate about lofty ideals, but if they are beyond your capabilities, troubles will arise. This is where devils will come to attack. For this reason, you have to use your wisdom and think about how to get your work done in a calm and objective manner.

People in the core positions of religion Are apt to be the target of devils' attacks

To fight against devils, strong reasoning power is required. Wisdom is also necessary. Devils do not study modern academic subjects, but they are quite intelligent because they were once leaders when they were alive. Devils that were former religious leaders can also talk about religious philosophies, so people can be deceived by their words. Devils' words mostly consist of the Truth with some misguided teachings mixed in, so people can be easily deluded. Devils that used to be Buddhist monks are well versed in Buddhist teachings, while devils who were Christian priests before falling to hell know well about Christianity. They are very knowledgeable about these doctrines, so people can be easily deceived.

Knowledge alone is insufficient to avoid being deceived by such devils; you also need a sharp intellect that is constantly being honed. If you are conceited, you cannot see through their false logic to defeat them. Devils can make very intelligent comments and even pretend to be angels, so you need to spot the slightest flaws in their arguments. Jesus Christ disputed with devils in this way, and so did Shakyamuni Buddha.

One of the Buddhist scriptures describes how a devil was constantly watching the Buddha for seven years as he was undergoing spiritual training. Like a crow expecting delicious food and hovering over a stone that resembled a piece of fat, the devil was always around. But just as the crow flew away after realizing that it was just a stone, when the Buddha attained enlightenment, the devil went away, depressed. We must be aware that devils are constantly roaming around on the lookout to target someone. Those who are in the core positions of religion are especially targeted by devils.

In Christianity, Judas betrayed Jesus, but it is understandable why this happened. Judas would agonize over matters related to money and women. Judas was in charge of collecting and managing the money for Jesus and his group of disciples. Those with such a duty should essentially work in the background, but given that Judas was in charge of managing money, he probably had a high ability in handling worldly matters.

Judas always had a hard time collecting money to supply the group's necessities, such as food. But Jesus was a free-spirited person and would suddenly start something new or make unexpected side visits to meet someone. As Judas tried hard to solidify the group, Jesus would often meet with people who had the potential to hurt its reputation. So, Judas would complain to Jesus and ask him to change his ways, just like a financial advisor would do today.

In the early stages, the group was small, but as it grew bigger, the number of its devoted believers also increased.

Then the long-serving disciples would start to feel as if their teacher had been taken away. Judas was indeed jealous of the new devotees. In addition, since the group grew to have a great influence in just a few years, his abilities probably could not keep up with the needed skills. When the group was still small, his role with financial matters may have been important to the group, but his position in the group may have eventually changed.

I can understand this situation very well. In Happy Science, too, many things happened during the first twenty years of our history. In the initial stages, devils would often enter the minds of our executives. They would possess a person for one to three months. So, in order to deal with this situation, I introduced the principle of impermanence into our management structure and made the organization more fluid. I made our organization highly flexible. After that, it became pointless to target our executives, and the devils became unable to possess them.

During the first few years, our executives were often targeted. When they failed to keep up in their abilities, they would be swiftly possessed. If I came to value someone as indispensable to Happy Science, that person would be targeted, so the more valuable the person, the more indifferently I had to treat that person. The person would be safe as long as I treated him or her less importantly, as if to say, "I don't care if you are here or not." But if he or she was considered irreplaceable, that person would be targeted and brought down for the smallest wavering of his or her mind.

So, I created a fast-changing organization and nurtured many executives so I would have enough capable staff ready for substitution. Then, devils stopped attacking our organization. It became pointless for devils to attack it because no matter how many people they brought down, there would always be others to replace the predecessors, resulting in each executive having less influence on the whole organization. Devils also consider work efficiency, and they do not work in vain. Thus, desires, including the desire for fame, are easily targeted, so we must fight using our wisdom.

A Sacred Rite for Exorcising Devils: "El Cantare Fight"

Create a spiritual screen by using the will of many

At Happy Science, "El Cantare Fight" is granted as one of the sacred rites to exorcise devils, and it is performed all over the world. The power of "El Cantare Fight" is closely connected to the daily spiritual discipline of the person who performs it. It means that the person must study the books of Truth, practice self-reflection, and recite prayers on a daily basis; the person must also follow certain self-set precepts and live in accordance with the Will of God or Buddha every day. The extent of such efforts and the power to exorcise devils are correlated. If you are diligently undergoing spiritual discipline, you can acquire and develop the spiritual power.

Happy Science holds ritual prayers to exorcise evil spirits at *shoja* (temples), such as the Head Temple Shoshinkan in Utsunomiya, Tochigi Prefecture. My disciples conduct these ritual prayers, and I have gone to see them for myself to make sure that devils were being properly exorcised. I confirmed that devils were indeed being dispelled.

It is good that they are dispelled, but sometimes they may move on to possess someone else, so this is a difficult matter. It would be great if they were expelled and disappeared on the spot, but sometimes they simply transfer to another person. To prevent transference from happening, we must increase our power as a whole. We must create a spiritual screen with stronger power, preventing devils from lingering. This is a matter of willpower, so it is better to perform the rite together, with many people rather than alone; in this way, the power will be much stronger. With many people focusing their power of thought on exorcising devils, the devils can no longer remain.

When exorcising devils, it is important to have the support of many people to create a spiritual field using willpower, leaving no room for devils. Whether you perform it at a local temple or shoja of Happy Science, make sure there is no area that is unguarded. So as not to allow devils to just move from one person to another, create a solid spiritual screen together with as many people as possible, and become united, as if to stand hand in hand and fight together.

It would be a problem if, while a ritual prayer was being performed in the prayer hall, a person cleaning the area outside suddenly became possessed by a devil as he turned toward the prayer hall. It is inexcusable if a devil simply transfers from one person to another as a result of performing exorcism, so we must create a perfect spiritual screen to cast devils out completely, leaving no room for them to stay. It is also necessary for people who take part in the ritual prayer to spend one or two hours in the spiritual field after the devil has gone. When performing exorcism, we need to take care to observe these points. Even so, I have confirmed that "El Cantare Fight" is effective in exorcising devils.

The spiritual meaning of the cross and star

In performing "El Cantare Fight," you use your hand or the Devil-Quelling Sword. First, you make the sign of the cross. In Christianity, you first move your hand from your forehead to your chest, then across your shoulders from left to right. In "El Cantare Fight," you first move your hand horizontally from left to right, and then vertically from up to down. We do the opposite of how Christians make the sign of a cross. Essentially, it does not matter how it starts, but I chose to do the horizontal line first to express that we are different from Christianity.

The sign of the cross has been used for two thousand years; it is a well-known symbol in the spirit world. The use of the sign gives a warning that God's power is at work. When seeing it, devils will prepare themselves. As the person praying makes the sign of the cross, a white light shines horizontally and then vertically. The possessing devil can see the light of the cross shining brightly, and it draws back.

Next, the sign of a star is made. The light of a star will also appear just the way you move your hand. A star is the symbol of victory and the symbol of heaven. The star represents a secret rite of heaven, as well as victory. Interestingly, Abe-no-Seimei, a Japanese spiritual leader of the Onmyodo (the Way of Yin and Yang) in the tenth century, also used the sign of the star to perform rituals. A star is referred to as a pentagram in the *I Ching* (Book of Changes), and it is used in Christian culture as well. In a religious sense, the sign of the star has power.

After making the signs of the cross and a star, lastly you move your hand or the Devil-Quelling Sword forward. In the middle of the palm of the hand, there is a chakra point from which great spiritual power is emitted. When you face your palm forward, a strong light comes out of your palm.

From the standpoint of a possessing devil, a cross appears, followed by a star, and finally a powerful light from the center of the star. Devils that receive "El Cantare Fight" feel crucified when the cross is made, and when the star is made they become paralyzed, being trapped by the spiritual screen. Being crucified on a cross and sealed inside a star, a light then emerges to strike the center of their hearts. This is how "El Cantare Fight" works.

Perform rituals with the light of El Cantare

Spiritual power will come from the *Gohonzon* (the object of worship), which is to say, the core consciousness of El Cantare, as long as the people performing "El Cantare Fight" have faith and are aware that they are doing it with the light of El Cantare. Light will come if they have faith, undergo spiritual discipline to purify their minds, and remain humble every day.

If you try to exorcise devils with your power alone, light will not flow; you need to remember that you are performing an exorcism with the power of El Cantare. If you think you can do it with your own power, a devil will enter your thoughts. So, you must think, "I am just a conduit or pipe that allows El Cantare's light to flow. The light of El Cantare comes out through me."

If you believe you are fighting devils with the light of El Cantare, devils will have no choice but to face El Cantare. But if you believe you are conducting exorcism with your own power, devils will see you as the enemy and come to attack you. In a one-on-one fight, you inevitably have some unguarded area, so you will most likely be defeated. Therefore, it is necessary to fight in unity with the entire organization. This is a fight we must do as an organization together with the heavenly world. The more spiritual training you accumulate every day, the stronger your spiritual power or Dharma power will be, and this will allow you to exert stronger power to exorcise devils.

Have a strong determination
To allow no more evil

Since devils have been in hell for one, two, or even three thousand years, it is nearly impossible for them to return to heaven through persuasion. A devil may be possessing someone, causing that person to say strange things, but it is useless to try and persuade the possessing devil. Devils try skillfully to cheat and deceive those who try to persuade them. They may even beg and cry, pleading, "Please save me," "I've changed my mind," or "Please let me be your disciple," but these are all lies so do not listen to them. Shedding fake tears is one of their techniques to deceive people.

Never negotiate with a devil. Just expel it. "Further evil shall not be forgiven. Evil shall never spread"—with such a strong will, exorcise it decisively.

Lost spirits that have not spent long periods of time wandering on earth can return to heaven through persuasion, but devils cannot, because they have done too much evil. So, you must rather prevent them from committing further evil. This is important.

Since it is impossible to eliminate devils altogether, I have adopted the policy of focusing our energy on enlarging the domain of Light and enclosing them. I am trying to create fortresses and bases of Light all around the world to surround the devils, gradually constricting their nesting places. It is a long battle, and since there are so many devils, we cannot win just by fighting unless Happy Science gains greater power.

But sure enough, devils do not cooperate with each other. This is most fortunate. It would be a greater battle if a large number of devils joined forces to attack at once, but they always fight on an individual basis. I truly appreciate this. I am not sure how many devils there actually are in hell—maybe hundreds or even thousands—and if they got together and attacked us all as one, it would be horrible. In reality, however, they cannot work together because when they do get together, they fight amongst themselves. So, they always appear individually. Devils never help one another or act cooperatively; they just work on their own.

Therefore, it is important for the forces of Light to have a common front and fight together hand in hand. Different devils will appear depending on the situation or their personal interests, but they attack at random, not in an organized way. That is why, if we fight as an organization, we can win.

If devils could also become united, they might be able to develop the feeling of fellowship and perhaps awaken to the feeling of love. But in reality, even if they tried to unite and form a group, it would not work because none of them would listen to one another. They can only be absolute dictators in a one-man show and cannot engage in an organized group battle.

When dealing with devils, never negotiate; just be determined not to allow further evil. Never listen to their fake words of regret or repentance. Do not get easily taken in by their "change of heart." This is not such an easy fight. It would take one or two thousand years for them to truly have a change of heart. Therefore, it is essential to be determined to prevent them from committing further evil and contain them with the force of Light.

To become a modern exorcist, you must put great importance on daily spiritual discipline. Even so, an exorcism conducted by a professional priest who has accumulated spiritual discipline, in a place such as a local temple, shoja, or headquarters where spiritual fields have formed, is most effective. In the case of ordinary believers, if they confront a strong devil and their spiritual powers are not strong enough to expel it, they can be defeated. Therefore, rather than doing an exorcism alone, it is better to have it conducted, if possible, by a professional priest at a Happy Science facility where there is a spiritual field.

In order for ordinary believers to strengthen their spiritual powers, they need to undergo similar spiritual discipline as professional priests. They also need to solve their personal troubles, get enough sleep and sufficient nutrition, and build their physical strength by managing their health. You cannot expel devils while managing many personal troubles, so it is important to clear away your personal problems. Ordinary believers can expel a simple low-level spirit, or one from their neighborhood, or one that perhaps followed their children home from school, by conducting "El Cantare Fight" at home, but in the case of a real devil, only professional priests can exorcise it.

6

Strengthen the Light
Rather than Focusing on Evil

Among those who help to carry out religious activities, there are some who become possessed by a devil despite not committing any serious wrongdoing. A devil enters through a wavering of their hearts and destroys their characters. As a result, they go mad and lose their lives in the end. Sometimes we see such pitiful people. It is very sad, but this cannot be helped.

This happens because devils approach these people with the clear intention of interfering with their work. I assure you that even if they were possessed by a devil and died miserably, they have actually returned to heaven in the afterlife. Their suffering is only in this world. Even if these people died while being possessed, after they move on to the other world they can return to heaven and live apart from devils. The outcome would be different for those who were possessed because of their wicked minds, but in the instance of those who have helped Happy Science but were destroyed by devils, I can guarantee their wellbeing in the next world, though they may have had to suffer some years before leaving this world. There is no need to worry.

There are indeed evil beings who commit themselves to wrongdoing, but it cannot be helped. We must rather strengthen the Light. Devils do not like self-reflection, prayer, humility, obedience, honesty, and faith. They will lose against such values, which are the exact opposite of worldly power. They can no longer possess people who adhere to these values. So, we must fight using these qualities.

As Happy Science grows larger and our local branches and shoja come to have a special spiritual atmosphere, our power of exorcism will increase. This being so, as I said earlier, we must fight using both the power of a spiritual field, or spiritual screen, and the power of an organization in which many people cooperate, uniting the power to create even greater power.

Nevertheless, after you have fought for a certain period of time, set aside the exorcism for a while, because if you focus too much on evil, you may sometimes lose. Do not fret over the weed that grows; just continue to sow good seeds to grow much wheat. More harvest is necessary to increase the Light. The weeds may bother you, but you must not pay too much attention to them. It is essential to increase the number of proper people, right people, pure people, and happy people. Time and again, remember to shift your attention in this way. This concludes my talk on the modern exorcist. I hope it will be helpful.

Chapter Two

Basic Measures to Overcome Spiritual Disturbance

From Basic Knowledge To Practical Application

Lecture given on September 5, 2018
at Special Lecture Hall, Happy Science, Tokyo, Japan

How to Identify Spiritual Disturbance

Everyone experiences spiritual disturbance Multiple times

I have already spoken on this chapter's theme many times in different ways, but I believe I need to speak on this topic repeatedly every year. It means we have to return to the basics of religion. While there are many subjects that can be covered by secular studies and professional work, this particular topic contains matters that are strongly related to religion. In this sense, I need to discuss ways of life that incorporate spiritual aspects, and how spiritual matters affect our lives. As suggested by its title, this chapter is intended to revisit basic knowledge.

Spiritual disturbance or possession by a spirit is actually not a unique experience. Everyone experiences it multiple times in life. So, when is it most likely experienced? Some examples are when your course of life has taken a different path from the one you wanted, when you are experiencing a deadlocked situation, or when you form bad associations through connections at work or activity groups. In such cases, it is quite difficult to escape spiritual disturbance.

For example, it might happen that you join a group of delinquent students through one of your friends and become unable to break away from the group. You will then be drawn into doing something bad at least once a day, as opposed to doing "one good deed a day." Each member takes a turn doing something wrong and when your turn comes you are also forced to do something bad. If you try to leave the group, you may be treated like a fugitive ninja from the olden days. It was said that when a ninja attempted to leave his group, he would be chased to death, and it is probably similar with this kind of group as well. In such circumstances, you will most likely be subject to spiritual disturbance.

The same is certainly true with criminal groups. If you join a group of people who band together to do wrong and commit crimes, you will gradually be soaked in evil. It is almost certain that evil spirits possess those who are engaged in illegal activity.

In Japan today, there is telephone fraud involving bank transfer scams targeting the elderly; a scammer posing to be a relative, often a nephew or a niece, calls the victim and asks for money, claiming, "It's me! I will be in big trouble if I don't get money right now. Please send money immediately." Apparently, some victims are even asked to bring cash to a nearby train station, though it is hard to believe that someone would fall prey to this kind of trick. I am not sure if the scammers actually check whether the victim has a nephew or niece, but they direct the victim to give the money to a go-between and in this way they carry out the swindle. There are sometimes fraud-warning notices posted publicly. It surprises me that such "businesses" actually exist.

If people are engaged in such criminal activities every day, their minds will be overshadowed by dark clouds. Their way of life is closer to that in hell, so they will be approached by evil beings through the Law of Same Wavelengths. Basically, this is the consequence for those involved in criminal activity.

Of course, what is considered a crime is different depending on the country. Some countries follow mistaken national policies, so in such countries, we cannot say that people who oppose the government are criminals and therefore possessed by evil spirits. Otherwise, if someone is engaged in work that is widely recognized as highly criminal, or is a long-term member of a criminal group, that person is most likely possessed by evil spirits.

Some newly formed religious groups or sects Have become nests of evil spirits

Religions are often disliked by the public, and there are good reasons for this. It is embarrassing to say this since I am in a similar vocation, but among the new religious groups and sects established in Japan between the end of the nineteenth century and the present day, some are indeed misguided or unacceptable in my eyes. In my case, for example, I am able to read through a type of encyclopedia on conventional religions, but I begin to feel ill when I read one on new religions. I assume it is because such an encyclopedia contains descriptions of groups that have obviously become nests of evil spirits.

There is a tendency for mass media today to evaluate all religions as one, at times approving of all or other times disapproving of all. This makes it difficult for us to comment on other religions. So, in the past few decades, there has been an unwritten rule for religions to refrain from criticizing each other, because when they do, the media targets both sides. All religions are lumped together, and their reputations rise or fall all at once, so this is a difficult matter. While Happy Science states that there are differences between religions, people have a hard time understanding this and are quick to conclude that all religions are the same in that they teach about supernatural matters.

Moreover, as an organization grows to a certain size, deviant individuals will appear in its membership. It is said that three out of a hundred Japanese may become criminals, and similarly, in a religion of a hundred followers, three or so criminals could naturally arise. If the number of followers increases to one thousand or ten thousand or more, a certain percentage of bad individuals will emerge. It would not be a big problem if it was only a slight misbehavior, but in cases where a follower commits a serious crime, the entire group could be dragged down. So this is a very delicate issue.

It is not easy to distinguish mental illness From spiritual disturbance

Similar problems can be viewed on the individual level as well. The Japanese law reports on one hundred selected judicial cases include the following case, in relation to freedom of religion and its limitations. A monk tried to exorcise a spirit—either a fox spirit or raccoon dog spirit—that he believed was possessing a person. With help from a family member of the afflicted person, he restrained and beat the person as he tried to expel the spirit. But because of the repeated beating, the person died and the monk was prosecuted.

If someone is truly possessed by an animal spirit like a fox spirit or raccoon dog spirit, he or she will often act in an odd way. This is obvious to those who closely observe the person. For example, the person may start to crawl on all fours or hop around. These are clearly abnormal behaviors, so those who are versed in religious matters will conclude that an animal spirit is possessing the person and take him or her to a psychic medium, where an exorcism might be performed. If the exorcism does not work no matter how many times it is performed, the exorcist may then start to inflict physical pain on the possessed person so the spirit in the body will feel uncomfortable enough to leave it. That is why sometimes exorcism can include some form of corporal punishment.

In films related to Christian exorcism, there are scenes in which a patient is seated and tied to a chair with leather restraints, like how a psychiatric patient is treated, and the exorcism is performed when he or she is unable to move. Just looking at the scene, you can hardly tell the difference whether one becomes violent because of a psychotic disorder or due to strong spiritual disturbance. In many cases, they overlap. For this reason, the Vatican has ruled that a patient must first be examined by doctors to see if he or she is mentally ill. If diagnosed to be ill, the patient would be sent to a hospital for psychiatric treatment. Exorcism is performed only after confirming that the behavior is not a symptom of illness. In reality, however, it is not so easy to distinguish between the two.

There is a well-known American movie, *The Rite*, in which actor Anthony Hopkins plays an exorcist. There is a scene where the subject is examined to see whether she is psychotic or possessed by a devil. She is tested to see if she has supernatural powers by having her guess what is in an opaque bag. This is the ability to perceive things without actually seeing them; in a broader sense, it is clairvoyance. In the movie, the girl guesses correctly that a dollar bill is in the bag, and the exorcist concludes that it is the work of a devil.

Other evidence in detecting spiritual possession is the ability to suddenly speak in tongues, foreign languages that the person should not know. There are also cases where a person can describe incidents in someone's past that he or she should not know. The person may say, for example, what someone's father said just before dying, how one's mother passed away suffering, or how a sibling is. Based on statements such as these, the exorcist will decide if the subject is possessed by a devil before performing an exorcism. However, these things can be very subtle to detect. It seems as if exorcists try hard to prove the existence of devils. A true spiritual expert can immediately identify whether a person is possessed or not.

Basic Knowledge Needed When Fighting Devils

Devils attack the weakest person of The target's closest relationships

Some people who have opened a spiritual pathway are quite susceptible to spiritual influence compared to ordinary people. These people are like houses with chimneys that allow Santa Claus to enter them. However, Santa Claus is not the only one that can enter; other beings can also come in. In addition, if a chimney is left unclean, Santa Claus can get dirty and cause a lot of trouble. In the same way, even if the person was in a good state of mind when his or her spiritual pathway opened, this state of mind can change and deteriorate if a serious incident occurs to put him or her in trouble. This will make things difficult.

Basically, there is the Law of Same Wavelengths for an evil spirit to possess a person, but there are also exceptional cases. An evil spirit or devil can put a person under intense spiritual disturbance or possession in order to cause suffering, not only to this very person it is possessing, but also to his or her family members such as siblings, parents, children, or those who work with the person. This style of indirect attack also exists.

In the game of Jenga, in which players take turns pulling out one of many wooden blocks that are stacked in layers, there is a tipping point when the whole structure falls down with the removal of one piece. In the same way, in a family unit or a group of people at work, there is a crucial point that can trigger the collapse of the whole if attacked. Devils basically use the same strategy as wolves hunting a flock of sheep. They target the weakest one and the easiest, most effective point of attack.

They hardly ever come in from the "front door." In most cases, they come in through a "back door." Usually people will not visit a house using a back door, but devils will. In fact, they will come through the relatives or acquaintances, the people that you know well and can hardly avoid or refuse. This is their basic approach. I have experienced this many times; their strategy is usually the same. They use the hunting style of a wolf and target the weakest. If there are several family members, they prey on the weakest one.

At school, bullying is often concentrated on the most vulnerable class member. Sometimes the easiest target is attacked to cause classroom disorder. If someone were to stand up against the bullies to help the friend who is being targeted, that person will be labeled as the same and targeted for bullying. The person is forced to be isolated so that he or she stands out from the rest. The isolated one will then fall into deep despair and gradually become unable to attend school. Such isolation can also happen at work or in the family; in many cases, it becomes quite difficult to restore the original relationships. In this way, devils sometimes target a specific person on purpose, and they are quite shrewd.

Appropriate measures for earth-bound spirits

Things are different with ordinary evil spirits. For example, in the case of earth-bound spirits that are associated with specific places, if you stay away from those particular places you will basically have no connection to them. But if you go to a graveyard just to test your courage, explore cemeteries to catch an eerie event on film, or frequent someone's grave, such spirits can very likely possess you. So, it is best to stay away from those places.

Some Happy Science facilities are located in areas with many traditional temples. Since there are many temples and graves nearby, I try not to visit or even view them on my way to our facilities. When we build facilities in such areas, we make sure that they are designed so there is no direct view of the graves from inside our buildings.

I have been living in my current residence for nearly twenty years now. Although there are many cemeteries in the neighborhood, fortunately I have had almost no visits from ghosts from the nearby graves. This is mainly because I make an effort to not create any direct ties with them. If I were to go to the cemeteries on my daily walks, spirits would probably visit me. Sometimes I have to pass by the Aoyama Cemetery on my way to visit places, but I try my best not to pay attention. If I walked past that spot every day, spirits there would be sure to approach me in time. Once they find that I am capable of communicating with spirits, they would want to interact with me and tell me their complaints.

As in the saying, "Far from Jupiter, far from his thunder," generally it is best to stay away from potentially dangerous places. Places where suicides are often committed are also dangerous. For example, these places can be railroad crossings or a section of a building from which people have jumped off.

The same is true with the so-called "stigmatized properties." Some properties that are rented or sold for great bargain prices may later turn out to be places where previous residents have hanged themselves. This is a familiar setting for TV dramas and horror movies, but my advice is to avoid buying or renting such a house or room. Sometimes you may have no choice, but otherwise, do not push yourself to test your courage; the rule of thumb is to avoid unnecessary contact.

People usually refuse to rent a property where the previous resident has committed suicide by hanging. In Japan, if a property has been rented out for a certain period of time after the fatal incident, it is no longer considered a "stigmatized property." That is why some real estate agents resort to false paper trails using the names of absent residents. They ask other agents to rent the property on paper only, claiming almost no rent for a certain period of time, perhaps six months or a year, to make it appear that someone has actually lived there. Then, after that period of time, the property is again put up for rent, and the agents no longer need to disclose the suicide incidents that occurred there. This kind of technique is sometimes used, so we need to be careful.

American horror movies often portray stories of haunted houses. For example, a ghost may inhabit a basement or a particular room where someone has died, and the person living there becomes possessed by the ghost, then by a devil that controls the ghost. There are many stories that follow this plotline. Many similar kinds of stories also exist in England. For example, a person finds an old relic in the basement that turns out to have belonged to someone who met a tragic death, or a person enters a room that has been locked since the death of a daughter and is then possessed by the girl's spirit. There are many such stories. It is best to avoid these types of places.

What exorcists learn in the Vatican

There are very few exorcists in the world who can expel possessing spirits. The Vatican reports that there are more than five hundred thousand requests for exorcisms made annually, but I estimate that very few are actually performed, due to the small number of Vatican-approved exorcists.

The Vatican offers an instructional course to produce official exorcists, but looking at the content of what is taught, I doubt the efficiency of their methods. I basically believe it is better not to know the names of devils, so I do not emphasize teaching their names at Happy Science, but the Vatican instructs priests to memorize their names. They even use illustrations depicting their faces and figures. I assume there are descriptions of about five hundred devils on the list, along with unique characters and features. I do not think it is necessary to memorize all the names and faces of devils to be certified as an exorcist. I doubt these details are based on the real observation, but such pictures are used.

The basic method of exorcism taught at the Vatican is as follows. First, they instruct the priests to bind the body of the subject suspected of possession to restrict his or her physical freedom. Exorcism involves danger because the subject might use extraordinary strength and become violent. They also instruct not to engage in conversation or listen to what the devils say. They even advise not to look directly into the eyes of the subject.

The rule for not engaging in conversation is portrayed in most exorcism-related movies. To make the stories more dramatic, many of the movies have scenes where a devil speaks with extravagant claims. At such times, devils usually use base language filled with many obscenities. They frequently use filthy expressions that would be considered taboo in normal workplaces and censored in broadcasting. Even a young girl who would not normally use such language will suddenly blurt out dirty, indecent slang words when under demonic possession.

They use such profanity partly because they want to agitate the mind of the priest performing the exorcism and distract his concentration. A priest about to sprinkle holy water or press a crucifix against the subject to perform the exorcism might wince when hearing so much vulgar language. Additionally, if he starts to argue on the same footing as the devil, his mental wavelength will gradually become attuned to that of the devil. That is why it is advised not to listen or converse with the devil.

These scenes are often depicted in movies, and they actually happen in real life. Even if someone outwardly appears to be a gentleman or lady, when the devil reveals itself, that person will suddenly start to verbally assault the priest with lewd words. Therefore, it is important to refine one's words. Being able to refrain from using vulgar language and using decent words means that your sense of reason is actually in control. This is worthwhile to note.

So, in a Christian-style exorcism, it is taught that one should not engage in any verbal battle or listen to what the devil is saying. Another instruction is to not look into the eyes of the subject. This is probably because eye contact can be used for hypnotic power to delude people.

In a related matter, I am somewhat skeptical of the efficacy of reading the Bible in Latin out loud, sprinkling holy water, and pressing a cross on the subject's face or body. These methods are portrayed in movies and dramas as part of the theatrical performance, but in reality, I doubt they are greatly effective.

Various traits of possession by devils

Some movies even show the phenomena of materialization. In the previously mentioned *The Rite*, for instance, a possessed pregnant girl throws up nails. The movie was advertised as being based on a true story, but I very much doubt that spitting out so many nails could actually happen. This must be an exaggeration of the movie.

The exorcist played by Anthony Hopkins is shocked by the death of the girl he was treating, and he later comes under demonic possession. When he becomes possessed, he too spits out nails from his mouth. I suppose the nails are symbolic of Christ being nailed to the cross. Although materialization phenomena do sometimes happen, it is an exaggeration to depict devils as having so much ability to materialize things or cause physical changes to happen. I find it a little problematic; it hardly ever happens in reality.

In most cases, those under demonic possession have a tendency to torment themselves. That is why they might attempt to hang themselves with a rope or cord around the neck, electrocute themselves, sprinkle gasoline and set themselves on fire, or jump out of a window. In other cases, they could turn violent against others, attempting to attack them with a knife if one is available. Therefore, it is necessary to keep things that could be used as weapons out of the way or hide them from sight.

It is also a problem if guns are kept near those with severe spiritual disturbance. It is better to put away any types of weapons such as guns and cutting tools; these items must be kept secured. It is also necessary to consider how to prevent suicidal jumping and poisoning by gas. Make sure to not allow easy access for such suicidal attempts. Liquids that can be ignited, such as gasoline or other flammable materials, are also dangerous. Take extra measures to keep them out of sight from these people.

In most cases, people with spiritual disturbance will rush toward self-harm. This is because they often hear the voices of the possessing spirit whispering, "Die, die, die" or "Jump off the building," into their ears or in their heads. These voices nag them constantly, making them unable to sleep at night, so they will gradually believe it is what they should do, as if in a hypnotic state.

In this sense, dangerous moments are when they feel emotionally low and feel it is the end of the world, such as when they get fired from a job, experience a broken heart, or fail an important test. One could feel deep shock by failing an examination to become a doctor and feel depressed, thinking, "I can never be a doctor. My parents will be disappointed. I would rather die." If at such a moment the person happens to be near a railway crossing like one of the previously mentioned suicide spots, that person could unwittingly wander into the crossing when a train is approaching.

Driving a car is also very dangerous for this type of person. While at the wheel, if one loses control of oneself for even a second, the person will allow the possessing spirit to move his or her hand to steer into danger, resulting in a collision or hitting a pedestrian.

In other cases, one may attempt to jump off a rooftop or out of a window of a tall building. But this is a matter of building design. If buildings have structures that allow no access to such areas, no one will die that way.

In the past, there were many people who committed suicide by jumping off platforms in front of trains. So recently, Japan Railways (JR Group) started to install access gates on platforms, which only open after trains have stopped. The JR Group had previously resisted installing these gates due to their high cost, but now many stations report no suicides. A train platform without gates is actually a very dangerous design; people with spiritual disturbance could easily jump off when tempted to commit suicide. So, we need to be cautious at these spots.

Thus, in many cases, devils first try to kill the person they possess or cause an accident. That is their tendency.

The differences between American and Japanese horror movies

As I said earlier, American exorcist movies often have scenes where the possessed character throws something up, like nails. Another familiar scene is the possessed person vomiting some gooey green substance. Maybe it was the idea of the art director or movie director to use pea soup. Certainly, the visual impact of some green substance being vomited is quite grotesque and helps create the sense of demonic possession on screen. In this sense, such an effect can work well.

In reality, however, it is unlikely. Even with my thirty-plus years of religious experience, I have never seen anyone vomiting any pea soup-like green substance. Of course, it is possible that people could get sick and throw up food they have eaten. It is certainly true that when people are under spiritual disturbance, their food preferences sometimes change, and they develop an aversion to certain foods. In that case, their body could reject such food and induce vomiting. Even so, there is no stereotypical case of vomiting a green substance. It almost never happens.

Another striking scene is a person's head turning 360 degrees, but that is impossible. If one's head turned 360 degrees, the neck would break, and the person would surely die. Therefore, this is also an exaggerated depiction. American exorcism-related movies use certain physical stunts to keep the audience riveted, so they tend to overdo these effects. That is what makes a box office hit in the U.S., but such a depiction would not be so popular in Japan.

Japanese ghost movies, on the other hand, take more of a psychological approach. Of course, they also show scenes that provoke fear in the audience, but not in a way that emphasizes physical action. That is why American horror movies often fail to gain popularity in Japan and might only be screened in a specific theater, whereas Japanese horror movies are rarely introduced in the U.S.

Some Japanese horror movies that make use of zombie-like characters, such as the series with the characters Sadako and Kayako, were remade in Hollywood as *The Ring* series and *The Grudge* series.

But those types of phenomena are not based on real experiences. Those filmmakers are probably quite unconventional and tried to use a unique approach. I have never seen or heard of dead people coming back to life as zombies to crawl around or attack the living in Japan. It is of course conceivable for the deceased to appear as ghosts and instill fear in people; they are quite capable of appearing in unbelievable forms.

There are certainly some physical phenomena related to the activities of poltergeists, such as mysterious noises, curtains moving without a cause, or lights turning off by themselves. But in Japan, it is very rare to observe this type of intense manifestation of physical phenomena. I think American horror films are basically more like murder mysteries that involve ghosts and devils. I have the impression that some murder cases are dressed up by adding ghosts and devils in the storylines. In reality, however, evil spirits and devils mostly target people's minds.

Practical Knowledge on Exorcising Devils

Listening to or watching Happy Science lectures

When a person comes under severe spiritual disturbance, even if the person does not possess any psychic ability, he or she will start to experience spiritual phenomena like a psychic does. More specifically, if evil spirits or devils constantly possess a person, he or she will become able to see spiritual beings or hear strange voices. This happens quite often. For example, if people are constantly being reprimanded at work, they will just want to cover their ears. At such times, they might hear voices whispering into them. If people experience this kind of auditory hallucination or clairaudience, they are most likely possessed by evil spirits or devils.

There are also times when one is suddenly overcome by drowsiness. There are of course times when one can feel sleepy all day long, which has nothing to do with spiritual influences, and I apologize if this might cause any misunderstanding. But still, a person can truly be overcome by a sudden drowsiness and be unable to stay awake, especially when starting to hear lectures of Buddha's Truth on CDs or DVDs. If you play a CD or DVD of one of my lectures for a person who has auditory hallucinations, the possessing spirit will try to prevent the person from listening to it, causing the person to fall asleep within five minutes.

When I worked at a trading company, I had a coworker who was possessed by a dog spirit. Surprisingly, this man had some knowledge of the spiritual world and asked me to expel the spirit, assuring me that he would keep it a secret. So, I responded to his request and had him listen to one of my Truth-related lectures, a spiritual message I had previously recorded on cassette tape. To my surprise, in less than three minutes, he fell fast asleep. Indeed, he immediately slumbered and was even blowing snot bubbles. I was amazed by the sudden reaction of the possession. He actually fell asleep all of a sudden when I played him a tape of one of my spiritual messages recorded earlier (now available in print). I was shocked by the instant effect. Thus, evil spirits and devils have the power to make someone fall asleep to prevent that person from listening to lectures on the Truth.

This also happens during my live lecture events. However, some people in the audience may fall asleep simply because they find the lecture boring. This cannot be helped at times. I do not want to overemphasize the sleeping aspect, because I am afraid that my disciples might accuse listeners who sleep during their lectures of being under demonic possession, when in fact their lectures are simply boring. In that case, they must improve their skills and make their talks more interesting. Nevertheless, it truly happens that some people begin to fall asleep as soon as they hear a talk on the Truth, so they are not able to listen to it.

Reading the books of Truth aloud

Now that the Happy Science Group has grown large, I am not directly involved in our daily activities and do not know about the details, but in our early days, I met people who had trouble understanding my books. They said that although they could recognize the printed words or see what was written, the message was not coming across clearly to them. Some said that no matter how many times they read my books, they just could not understand or absorb the content, while others said that they could not read the text because it appeared to quiver. This is exactly the same problem as not being able to listen to my lecture, as I just explained. There are also cases of being unable to read my books.

There are of course exceptions because some people may hate reading and just be unable to read any long, serious material. I myself am the opposite; I have trouble reading current popular novels. This may make my point a little complicated, but I just cannot understand what some current writers are trying to say—their stories are not clear and make no sense to me, and I have no clue about the purpose or message of their writing.

Nevertheless, there are cases where a person is not able to read any books published by Happy Science. If you suspect someone might be under spiritual disturbance, have him or her read aloud just one page of a book, such as *The Laws of the Sun* (New York: IRH Press, 2018) or *The Rebirth of Buddha* (Tokyo: Happy Science, 2009). You can tell if people are under spiritual disturbance if you have them read a page or two. If indeed they are under negative spiritual influence, they will soon become unable to read aloud. Such people cannot read my books, or even if they can, they cannot listen to my lectures. Generally, it is easy to tell because they will start to act violently or behave in a strange manner.

Going to a local branch of Happy Science

Those people will also resist going to a local branch of Happy Science. When people say they are afraid of crossing the threshold of a Happy Science branch, sometimes it is not because they are simply cautious of religion in general, but because they feel hesitant as a result of spiritual disturbance. For example, when a person joins Happy Science and invites his or her family members to visit the local branch, some may resist going there. Sometimes it is due to their natural disposition or their intellectual skepticism telling them not to go, but in many cases, it is because the spirits possessing them loathe to go there.

This can happen even at a lower spiritual level, such as at local traditional temples or shrines, which have nothing to do with my lectures or books. Recently there has been an increasing number of pilgrims visiting my hometown, Kawashima in Tokushima Prefecture. I attended Kawashima East Nursery School, which was located on the side of a slope that stretched from the Kawashima Shrine down to its outermost Torii gate. I do not have much knowledge about the god enshrined in the Kawashima Shrine; maybe it is not a well-known deity. But it is a proper shrine with a Shinto priest working there, and it probably has some spiritual power. In my childhood, I heard the following story about the Kawashima Shrine from my mother.

The existence of *Inugami* (literally, a dog deity) is widely believed in Tokushima, and it is said that it sometimes possesses living people. One day, an old neighbor woman who was suspected of Inugami possession was taken to the Kawashima Shrine. After passing through the Torii gate, she suddenly got down on all fours and started walking on her hands and knees. I am not sure if the Kawashima Shrine truly has such spiritual power, but perhaps Inugami is similar to an animal spirit and simply did not want to be taken to a true "god." I have heard many such stories of spiritual phenomena, so it may well have some power.

Listening to the CD of my recitation of The True Words Spoken By Buddha

I believe all spiritually sensitive people at Happy Science listen regularly to the CD of my recitation of our basic sutra, *The True Words Spoken By Buddha*. They also

The CD of *The True Words Spoken By Buddha*   *The True Words Spoken By Buddha*

probably listen repeatedly to my lectures on CD. When they suspect they are coming under spiritual disturbance, they most probably fight against it by listening all night long on headphones to the CD of *The True Words Spoken By Buddha* or to one of my lectures.

Of course, this is very effective in dispelling evil spirits and devils. If the spiritual disturbance is not so deeply rooted, just listening to the CD of *The True Words Spoken By Buddha* or to one of my lectures would be enough to expel them. But it would be difficult if the person's soul itself is rotting or becoming malignant, because the possessed and the possessing spirit already share the same qualities in considerable amount. If, like food that has passed its expiration date, one's mind starts to go bad, it will attract "flies," and they will not scatter no matter how hard one tries to shoo them away. That is because it is the rotten part of the soul that is attracting the flies. In that case, the playing of the CD of *The True Words Spoken By Buddha* alone cannot dispel the "flies" that are drawn to the "rotten food."

I am saying this based on my various experiences and knowledge of all situations; sometimes exorcism does not work when a considerable part of a person's "inside" is rotten. It is similar to a tooth cavity, for example. A cavity is repaired by removing the decay and then capping it with gold or other materials, but if the decay progresses under the cap and the tooth is damaged at its root, the total affected area must be treated.

Countermeasures for people
Who cannot practice self-reflection

Unfortunately, those suffering from severe spiritual disturbance basically cannot practice self-reflection because they do not always remember their thoughts and deeds. Or they tend to feel self-pity or easily succumb to self-denial, and fiercely resist any introspection. That is why, in most cases, they cannot practice self-reflection.

In the case of a person who is capable of doing self-reflection when advised, just listening to the CD of *The True Words Spoken By Buddha* would probably be enough to dispel the possessing evil spirit. However, those who are deeply invaded by evil spirits cannot reflect on their thoughts and deeds and instead blame everyone around them, insisting that they are not at fault. In such cases, listening to one of my lectures or playing a CD of our sutra alone is not enough to expel possessing evil spirits. In fact, the minds of the afflicted are closer to those of evil spirits, and that is why evil spirits cannot be easily removed from them.

They will always say, "I am not to blame. That person is at fault. The circumstances were against me. It is the fault of those around me." They repeatedly blame others and the environment in this way. This is a human weakness; everyone has this trait. For example, sensitive people will always say these things to avoid feeling hurt. Others may feel injustice when their opinions or ideas are not accepted. So, everyone more or less experiences these feelings.

The question is whether these feelings are within a reasonable, commonly acceptable range or are too extreme. Of course, there are people of conviction, who stick to their ideas and act on strong beliefs, in positions of leadership. Otherwise, some people are like old houses with rotten pillars that can hardly withstand any typhoon or hurricane. Even if some protective measures are taken on the outer part of the house, it is not easy to prevent a house with a rotten foundation from collapsing. For such cases, it will be a harsh battle.

For this reason, there are actually times when you cannot save a person despite your efforts at exorcism. Sometimes it is too late because the person has been immersed in evil spiritual influence for too long. In most cases these people have been contaminated since childhood, growing up in a family environment where evil spirits were present, and the parents also displayed the tendency to blame others and external factors. Naturally, the children will be affected by it. Of course, it is natural that children have conflicts with their parents, but under such parental influence they mostly end up becoming unable to practice self-reflection.

If you are dealing with people who do not like to follow moral obligations and refuse to practice self-reflection, you can at least provide them with some knowledge of Truth so they have something to think about. This is important. People cannot deepen their thoughts without any materials to consider, so it is necessary to give them things to contemplate and help them deepen their thoughts little by little.

It is also difficult to treat these people who are not able to listen to my lectures or read my books. In such cases, you can take an easier step by offering simple words of wisdom or indirect advice. Sometimes those are the only measures you can take. Some people cannot really be helped unless they experience some kind of terrible setback, where they fail miserably as if falling hard, face first. Some may not change even then, but others will certainly become more or less aware of their mistakes through such an experience.

Tendencies of people
Whose souls originally came from outer space

Though this may not necessarily be related to spiritual disturbance, I have discovered certain characteristics of those whose souls had come from the Pleiades* through my various Space People Readings†. There are of course several stars in the Pleiades star cluster, and I am not sure if all beings from there have the same characteristics. Nevertheless, according to our analysis of several souls of Pleiades origin, the society they come from is apparently based on a class system.

While I cannot make a definite statement, its society seems to consist of about 20 percent of the population in the upper class and the other 80 percent working to support the upper class. That seems to be how the society runs. Those who have so far appeared in our Space People Readings mostly belong to the upper 20 percent, and we have not found many of those belonging to the supporting class. Therefore, we have a risk of forming the wrong image of the Pleiades stars by basing our information on just the upper-class people.

However, one thing that is certain about the Pleiades social system is that it is not a money-based economy. They

---

* Translator's Footnote: The Pleiades are an open cluster in Taurus. Humanoids that are physically similar to Western people reside there. They value beauty and love, and can use magic and healing power.

† TF: There are people on Earth who have come to inhabit Earth from outer space. Okawa has the ability to trace back to the old memories of a person's soul and call upon his or her consciousness that used to live in outer space. The conversation with such a consciousness is known as Space People Reading. There are also space people that are currently visiting Earth on UFOs, and the conversation with such space people is called UFO Reading. Okawa also conducts UFO Reading.

do not seem to have the idea that people should engage in work to get paid for their labor and live within the means of their earnings. In fact, the class they are born into determines their lifestyle, and those born into royalty or other high-ranking families automatically expect others to provide them with offerings or tribute. They are like the landholders of feudal times; they do not farm the land themselves but have tenant farmers who work their land, and they receive part of the harvest as offerings from the tenants.

There are also people like royal princesses and those who value an academic background or physical appearance. If what they assert is put in the modern context, they claim that they deserve the service of others because they have a good academic background and are clever, or that they should be treated differently from others because they are so highly attractive or good-looking. In this way, some insist that others should work for or serve them. From this we came to understand that they do not have a monetary economic system.

These star people from the Pleiades came to Earth a long time ago and landed in Japan and other countries. At that time, many probably claimed themselves to be gods. These people have a strong tendency to negate labor or anything to do with finances. We have come to understand this about their character. In this sense, the people of Pleiades origin show a tendency to make light of diligence, hard work, and effort. There are also the types of people who have strong self-confidence and cannot practice self-reflection, and who want to be treated differently from other people.

There seems to be yet another type of people of Pleiades origin; they have developed a foxlike tendency, taking pride in cheating other people. There are many Japanese folktales of foxes or raccoon dogs playing tricks on people. It is unclear if they are based on true stories, because we do not see foxes and raccoon dogs tricking people today, and the old folktales are a jumble of stories from mixed sources. The stories could actually be about ghost-like animal spirits, or human spirits who had fallen to the Hell of Beasts and came to possess foxes or raccoon dogs to delude people. But another possibility is that the Pleiadians with a cunning character turned into foxes, while nonorthodox people from the star Vega* turned into raccoon dogs. Vegan star people have the power to transform themselves, and some may exhibit their ill-nature by deception, trickery, and doing mischief to others. In any case, it is worthy to note that certain souls have such tendencies.

---

* TF: Vega is the first-magnitude star in Lyra. Vegan star people can change their appearances at will depending on who they make contact with. There are three genders to them; male, female, and neuter. They have highly advanced scientific technologies and healing power.

Among people of Pleiades origin, those who are good-looking, intelligent, or from elite families tend to become *tengu* (long-nosed goblins), swelling with pride. Some of the Vegan star people who have wickedness in their hearts may also manifest as tengu. Those of Andromeda constellation origin[*] usually have the tendency to fight for justice, but if they become intoxicated with their own power, they could also become tengu. Those of Centaurus constellation origin[†] are mostly proud of their intelligence and advanced science, so many of them seem to have a tendency to believe in scientific abilities or develop materialistic thinking. Some people have such mistakes in their souls, and their core belief does not accord with the Happy Science teachings, so it is important to be aware of these possibilities as well.

---

[*] TF: Andromeda is a spiral galaxy which is about 2.5 million light-years from the Milky Way Galaxy. It is about twice as large as the Milky Way. It is said that Andromeda Galaxy is now moving toward the Milky Way at about one hundred kilometers (about sixty-two miles) per second, and is expected to collide with the Milky Way in around 4.5 billion years.

[†] TF: Centaurus is a "star of intelligence" where scientific technology is highly advanced. Okawa's Space People Reading has so far confirmed Alpha Centauri, Beta Centauri, and Theta Centauri. It is said that various species of space people inhabit the constellation.

The Techniques of Deceit
Used by Devils and Misguided Religions

Only truly spiritually awakened people
Can identify devils

As described earlier, in a Christian-style exorcism, the exorcists learn the names of devils. Their basic strategy is to force the possessing devil to say its name by means of pressing a crucifix up against the body, sprinkling holy water over it, and reading the Bible aloud. After they succeed in having the devil reveal its name, nearly half of the work of exorcism is done because a devil will flee when its name is revealed. This is the fundamental logic.

This is true to a certain degree. Taking Japanese folktales from the earlier example, the spirit of a raccoon dog or fox can possess living people, or they can make themselves appear in different forms, but what happens if their mischief is detected? For instance, when what appears to be a beautiful woman or a Buddhist monk is identified to be a raccoon dog or fox in disguise, it will swiftly revert to its original form. This happens because once its identity is made clear, it will lose its spiritual power and can only flee, unable to remain. This can be the case at times, so revealing the names of devils can sometimes be effective.

However, devils can easily lie to those who are not truly spiritually awakened—that is to say, those who do not have spiritual enlightenment. While exorcism movies may use made-up gimmicks like vomiting pea soup and spitting nails out of one's mouth, devils are truly liars and often talk nonsense. When a priest cries out a possible devil's name, the devil will easily affirm it, even if it is not true. In this sense, the method of revealing names is somewhat questionable.

I once saw a TV program reporting on a Catholic priest conducting an exorcism in a country in South America. He, seemingly a Spaniard, was treating several women who claimed to have been feeling unwell due to demonic possession. When performing an exorcism, he yelled out the name of a devil and exclaimed, "Get out!" as he rolled the woman's body on the ground.

However, the place seemed to be a typical farming village, and it is extremely unlikely that a notorious devil, the kind that appears on the Vatican's list, would possess an ordinary farmer. The priest called out the particular name of a devil to perform the exorcism and claimed to have finally cast it out, but devils are actually too busy to be involved in a matter that would only have a small effect. They would rather attack a subject whose fall would have greater impact; in modern days, the target would be an influential person, or a key person who could trigger a chain of events to cause destruction in other places as well.

Anyone can certainly fall ill or feel unwell due to some negative spiritual influence, but ordinary people would not normally be targeted by a powerful devil. In this sense, the basic logic of Christian exorcism—that the disclosure of the name of a devil will lead to dispelling it—is incorrect. Low-level spiritual mediums cannot usually detect what kind of spirit is possessing a person. The possessing spirits will often lie, and if the mediums believe them they could be deceived. Spiritual mediums must always remain humble because they often mistake the identity of the possessing spirit. They need to be well-versed in the techniques of the devils' deceptions and lies. There have been many spiritual mediums who were unable to tell good spirits from bad, but having believed their spiritual revelation to be true, they went on to start their own religious groups, only to end up misguiding other people. So, please be careful.

Mistakes of religions
That emphasize ancestral memorial service

Sometimes devils, demons, or evil spirits pretend to be an ancestor of the person they possess. They make their appearance and may claim themselves to be a deceased father, mother, grandfather, grandmother, or sibling. There are a lot of religious groups that frequently conduct ancestral memorial services, but many have become like "factories producing evil spirits" and attract many spirits that are not one's direct ancestors or relatives.

Needless to say, conducting memorial services for ancestors to help them awaken to the Truth is an important religious practice for those who sincerely lead the life of Truth. However, there is a problem if it is conducted while people have blame in their hearts toward others or blame the circumstances for their bad luck. There are, for example, religious groups that teach, "You are not at fault. The deceased father (or mother, grandfather, grandmother, elder sister, young brother, or other) is still lost and brings you misfortune. That is the source of your unhappiness, but you can find salvation through ancestral memorial service," or "You must sever ties to your ancestor's karma to become happy."

One of the esoteric Buddhist sects teaches that one should break away from the karma of one's ancestors by reciting a particular sutra daily for a period of one thousand days while rubbing Buddhist prayer beads together in both hands. Another sect puts all blame on the parents, saying, "Only by cutting all connection to your parents' karma will you succeed at study and work, and find a good marriage partner."

There are certainly parents that children may feel ashamed of, perhaps because they lacked an education, had a poor appearance, misbehaved in some manner, had a bad reputation, or failed in business. Some religious sects use this as an opportunity and say, for example, "Your parents failed in business because there is 'bankruptcy karma' in your family. If you break off from this karma, you can be successful in your own business," and some people are easily deceived by such talk.

In reality, it is not because of "bankruptcy karma" that one fails in business. There is no such karma; it is the matter of how you think. Whether your business succeeds or not depends on your way of thinking, knowledge, and experience. This is how some religious practices are actually misused.

Deceit used by religions
That teach Light-Only Thinking

To people who experience a series of mishaps such as becoming ill or a death in the family, some religious groups preach, "All bad incidents are signs of good things to come. You may feel you are facing the worst time, but it is just the process of bad things dissolving called the 'chemicalization of fate.' So, everything will be better from now on." But there is a certain deception in this thinking as well.

When bad incidents happen consecutively, in most cases there are reasons for them, so we must essentially find out the causes and remove them. Just stating that everything will change for the better is indeed a false claim. It would be more pleasing to encourage those who come for advice by only focusing on positive aspects and saying that all bad things have passed and things will only get better. However, there can be some deception even with this kind of Light-Only Thinking, and misguided religions abuse this thinking.

Checkpoints for Preventing Oneself From Coming under Spiritual Disturbance

The basic approach is correcting Your mind and your lifestyle

As stated earlier, ancestral memorial service can be used to deceive people. There are techniques of deception in which people are told, "You can be happy if you break away from all your ancestors' karmas once and for all," or "Disown your child to break the parent-child bond, and then you can be happy." Please do not be fooled by such talk.

The primary principle is always the same: Direct your thoughts in the right direction and correct your life every day. This is important. In simple words, it means to do one good deed a day and speak rightful words. If you have made a mistake in your relationships, admit your mistake and apologize for it if it is not too late. In this way, reflect on your thoughts and deeds and correct your way.

If, for example, you have bullied someone, apologize to the other party for your wrongdoing and your mistaken thoughts. Or if, in the workplace, you feel remorse for lying and blaming others for mistakes you made that caused trouble for the company, confess your mistakes honestly and apologize from your heart. If you do this, evil spirits cannot possess you for long. This may seem like basic moral behavior, but my advice is to start with such simple actions.

The recitation of Happy Science's basic sutra, *The True Words Spoken By Buddha*, and listening to my lectures are effective only when you direct your mind in a good direction, determined to rebuild yourself and to stay away from negativity. If, in the opposite manner, you seek an easy way out to be saved, or only try to solve spiritual trouble with an egotistical motive, unfortunately salvation will not be possible in many cases.

Basically, when people are possessed by evil spirits, they frequently abuse others verbally or speak ill of others; they blame others and do not reflect on themselves. What is more, as mentioned earlier, those possessed by devils will use a lot of obscene and vulgar language and insult the actions of priests. In this way, they try to hurt the priests' minds. They try to upset priests and disturb their concentration. These are traits you need to check and see.

Incidentally, according to my recent research on space people, concentration of the mind is essential even for space people. I have learned that when their concentration is disrupted, their spaceships could crash. The operation of UFOs is actually quite simple compared to earthly spacecrafts. Their mechanical systems are closely linked to the pilots' mental activity and concentration, and their equipment is created to be in tune with the wavelengths of the pilots' minds. In simple words, UFOs are operated telepathically. Since the UFOs operate while sensing the thoughts of the pilots, they could crash if the pilots come under spiritual disturbance. If the pilots are not in good condition and disembark, their UFOs can no longer fly. Thus, concentration of the mind is an ability that is highly involved in future science as well. This is worthy to note.

Change your mind
To be completely free of spiritual possession

This chapter has covered some basic knowledge of spiritual disturbance while incorporating some new topics. When you are satisfied with yourself for having gained much experience and achieved greatness, you tend to neglect your basic effort. Therefore, always remember your initial aspirations.

The dangerous signs of possession are, for example, that you cannot read any books of Buddha's Truth, watch any of the DVDs or listen to CDs of my lectures, recite Happy Science sutras, or listen to the chanting of the sutras. You feel like resisting strongly, running away, covering your ears, or you may be unable to sleep at night. If you observe these signs, please be careful. Things cannot change quickly, but strive to make things move in a good direction little by little.

It is also important to make the habit of visiting a Happy Science local branch or shoja. Some of you may believe you can study the Truth by yourself at home, but you will often end up being a self-styled practitioner. Exchanging ideas with others who study the Truth and learning from their advice are also valuable.

I also recommend that you attend one of my public lectures. Then you can find out for yourself whether you are currently under spiritual disturbance. During my lecture, if you feel the Light going deep into your heart, you are facing in the right direction. However, if you feel like something is covering your ears and you cannot hear my lecture, feel isolated as if surrounded by aliens, or feel uneasy, it is highly likely that you are possessed by some negative spirit. If, by any chance, you fall asleep and form a snot bubble during my lecture, it could be a sign of a more serious problem. In any case, you are suspected of being under spiritual disturbance if you cannot clearly hear or understand the critical part of the lecture that is particularly sensitive for you. You will be able to test yourself in this way, so I advise that you occasionally attend my lectures.

It can of course happen that the possessing spirit would be "blown away" by the power of my lecture. Sometimes my talk will bring you such benefit, but usually the possessing spirit will soon return unless you change your mind. It has such a nature, and the law of inertia will continue to work until you correct your way. For example, a train running at high speed will not suddenly stop even if the brakes are applied; it will keep going for a few hundred meters. Likewise, the tendencies of one's mind will not stop immediately. This is how it works.

This concludes the message on basic measures to overcome spiritual disturbance. I hope you will make good use of this knowledge.

Chapter Three

The Real Exorcist

The Power to Ultimately Win Against the Devil

Lecture given on May 9, 2018
at Special Lecture Hall, Happy Science, Tokyo, Japan

Not Many People Can Teach Real Exorcism

Many people need to awaken to the right path

As the chapter title indicates, I intend to talk about how to be a true exorcist, a master who can exorcise evil. I have already spoken on this topic several times in the past, and I have published *Akuma-kara-no-Boei-Jutsu* (literally, "The Way to Defend Yourself from Devils")(Tokyo: IRH Press, 2017), *Basics of Exorcism* (Tokyo: HS Press, 2015), and *Shinjitsu-no-Reinosha* (literally, "The True Spiritual Medium")(Tokyo: IRH Press, 2017). I have also given an English lecture with the same title, *The Real Exorcist*, and published it with its Japanese translation on the opposite page (Tokyo: Happy Science, 2017). I believe it is necessary to continually address this topic because there are variations of it, and confusion and misunderstanding may arise when different types and forms of spiritual possession are involved.

Not many people can teach exorcism. In Christianity, Jesus Christ exorcised devils; but for two thousand years afterward, I presume no one could correctly teach it. Even so, a certain methodology for exorcism seems to have been established after some exorcists had some success in exorcising devils. Horror movies and other Western-style exorcism movies clearly show a fixed style. However, I am somewhat doubtful of how much they understand the truths behind exorcism.

The same is true with Buddhism. Some monks may have clearly understood how exorcism worked, whereas others did not. The founder of the Shingon sect of Buddhism, Kobo-Daishi Kukai [774–835], for example, most probably had a very good understanding of exorcism. He knew much about how to dispel or quell evil spirits and devils. He also probably understood the kind of discipline and enlightenment that would be necessary to do so. But there were others who resorted to easy methods and did not seem to truly understand exorcism. It is very difficult to judge exorcism in a historical perspective.

In modern contexts, it is true that newly established religious groups are often disliked. Happy Science is no exception, and we have sometimes become the subject of criticism. One of the reasons the public dislikes so-called new religions is the negative changes in their followers. If a religion truly receives power from angels, God, or Buddha, it will emanate a holy or purifying atmosphere. But after joining a particular religious group and participating in its activities, some followers undergo some negative changes in their behavior or character. In many cases, their family and friends would advise them that they should quit.

There are also religious groups that are totally caught in the devil's net. Some of them have grown into fairly large organizations, and unfortunately, there is almost no hope for them to be saved. Some groups declare that they have hundreds of thousands or even millions of followers but have fallen into the hands of devils. Since they have so many followers, there even are specific areas in hell to which their followers go after death. It is not easy to rescue those people from there.

While alive, you have the chance to either walk on the right path or the wrong one, and it is essential that more people awaken to the right path.

2

Places Where Lost Spirits are Likely to Appear

Lost spirits will cause disturbance
The longer they linger on earth

In the Happy Science movie, *Twiceborn* (Executive Producer and original story by Ryuho Okawa, scheduled for release in fall 2020), there is a scene in which the main character conquers a devil and attains enlightenment. It is indeed very difficult to exorcise devils in real life.

Many people neither believe in the other world nor understand spiritual sensitivity. These people tend to scorn any spiritual matters. Among them, I suppose, are scientists, doctors, philosophers, and regular business people. For this reason, the majority of society often considers spiritual matters "silly stories." In reality, however, the power of spirits is truly at work.

In general, the souls of the deceased that are confused and do not know where to go after death are called "lost spirits." In a broader sense, they could be classified as "evil spirits." They are unable to return to heaven and wander around the earth. If these spirits linger on earth for a long period of time, they will start causing disturbances. In fact, since they had no knowledge of the world after death and did not even believe in the afterlife, they have no place to go. That is why they stay around their family, friends, or workplace acquaintances, or they remain in their homes or on specific lands. This will then give rise to various spiritual phenomena, causing misfortunes to those involved. These incidents happen often.

Lost spirits wander around Particular places or family

A common trait of Japanese and Western horror or exorcism-related movies is that evil spirits haunt a specific place. An evil spirit that has some connection to a certain location will appear and curse the people there. A typical pattern is a family moving into a house and one or more of the family members being confronted by an evil spirit. The spirit of a person who was murdered or met with a tragic death in the house usually inhabits it; the spirit is still lost and feels a strong attachment to the place.

Compared with Japanese movies, Western movies seem to have more stories involving houses, perhaps because of the greater permanence of Western buildings. In the West, there are many strong, stone houses that have lasted over one or even two hundred years, and older buildings usually have higher economic value. If a building is considered to be "haunted," its value can increase even more. In the U.S., which is still a young country, "haunted houses" are perceived as historic and traditional buildings, and these houses are said to be worth more, depending on the buyer's taste. In England, it is said that ghosts appear in most castles and prices are higher for haunted houses. In Japan, on the other hand, houses are much less permanent and we rarely see ancient houses. That is probably why Japan has fewer stories involving houses than the West. However, there still are a few stories about specific places that were sites of suicide or murder.

It is common in Japan and other countries for a guest to be confronted by a spirit of a deceased while staying in a hotel where a murder or suicide took place. The spirit can then possess the person because of their connection to the location. The same can happen at schools. If, for example, a student was killed or committed suicide due to bullying or physical abuse, the spirit sometimes lingers around the school because the student did not learn about the afterlife or the parents have not come to guide the spirit. It remains as a child and tries to entice other students with similar mindsets who are bullied and feel like committing suicide. There are actually such spirits, and such accounts are often told in school ghost stories. These spirits are associated with a specific place.

The spirits of one's deceased family members could also become lost spirits, and it is difficult to avoid this kind of relation. If, for example, a family member, such as a parent, grandparent, or sibling, passes away and their spirit becomes lost, it basically relies on bereaved family members for help. The spirit comes to them either because it knows about the other world and wants to be saved or because it knows nothing about the other world and has nowhere else to go. Everyone is spiritually sensitive to a certain degree, so if your deceased family member has become a lost spirit and is possessing you, you will feel somewhat unpleasant. You may also find yourself shunned by others or find that your work is not going well.

There are many such cases, so we must cut off the source of supply of lost spirits. That is why I teach, "Human spirits originally live in heaven in the other world, but we will eventually choose our parents to be born into this world. We lead our lives on earth and, depending on our thoughts and deeds during our lifetime, our lives will be judged either as good or bad, determining our destination after death. Such a system is in place." But since we cannot see or touch the other world or spirits, people find it hard to believe.

Spirits involved in the Ouija board game

Some Western movie plots make use of the Ouija board; the main characters try to communicate with spirits through the Ouija board, but as they play with the indicator pointing to the letters on the board, they become possessed by a devil. This type of story pattern is quite common.

In Japan, there is a similar activity called "Kokkuri-san," which uses a coin and a board printed with Japanese syllables, numbers, a Torii mark, and marks for yes and no. The spirits summoned during such a game are mostly animal spirits and it is very rare for powerful devils to come and possess a person playing it. In the West, houses often have basements that might have been used to perform rituals for calling out spirits of the dead, and perhaps the lost spirits that had some connection to those locations would still be there and guide the devils in.

Initially, a lost spirit or evil spirit of a family member or a person who had some connection to the place would come and possess a person playing the game. But if the person turns out to be the type that can cause a bigger problem in society or spread unhappiness to others, he or she would then be approached by a much stronger one, and be utilized as its tool or an "effective weapon." There are also people who are fascinated by spiritual matters, but if they thoughtlessly get too involved, more and more spirits will pay them visits. As they deepen their interest, "stronger ones" might gradually "awaken" and make an appearance. This is where we should be very cautious.

At schools, children might play "Kokkuri-san" and when they place their index fingers on the coin, they may find that it moves automatically to create some message on the board. But as they continue playing, the messages may gradually become dark and eventually spell out, "die" or "jump out of the window," which would frighten the children. Such incidents are sometimes reported in the society pages of newspapers. That is why the game is often banned at schools.

3

The Principle of Spiritual Possession And Its Real Situations

Spirits in hell will possess those With a similar tendency of the mind

Different kinds of spirits will come to possess people, but those involved in religious activities can be the target of not only the spirits of deceased family members and acquaintances but also real devils. There are indeed many kinds of enemies. A major battle is taking place over the right to control the earthly world—the battle between heaven and hell.

From the perspective of hell, the world on earth looks like the sea where children are playing on boats and rubber rafts with sharks swimming in the shallow waters just below. Evil spirits are just like the sharks circling below the surface while waiting for any children who might go overboard. This is how close the distance is between this world and hell.

Among the spirits in hell, some have totally become devils after spending long periods of time in hell. Others that have not spent so many years in hell after death—about fifty to one hundred years—still have attachments to the life on earth. So they seek a chance to have access to the earthly world, and when they find someone whose mind shares a common trait with theirs, they possess that person. While under possession, they can temporarily escape the suffering of hell and satisfy their desires to live as humans.

They usually cannot continue possessing a person for a long time; they can only do so for limited hours in a day. If they cannot possess the person during the day, they come at night, when everyone has fallen asleep. They target the person and cause sleep paralysis or nightmares in the middle of the night or at dawn. They may make the person suffer nervous sweats or sometimes cause poltergeist phenomena to occur. It is a rough ordeal for the person who is possessed.

The reason spirits in hell possess people on earth

What, then, does the phenomenon of spiritual possession signify?

Some Western movies regarding devils are based on the idea that a devil can be born as a human infant, as seen in *Rosemary's Baby*. In *The Omen*, a devil is born as a baby with the number 666 imprinted on his scalp. However, if devils and evil spirits were to be allowed to enter a mother's womb and be completely reborn as a human, there would be no need for them to possess people who are alive. Once in a physical body, they would be released from hell. In reality, however, this is not possible, and that is why they possess people on earth. This is my basic idea concerning spiritual possession.

It is extremely difficult for a spirit in hell to enter a mother's womb. Spirits cannot be born on earth unless they regain a certain level of serenity of the mind and raise their spiritual vibrations to the heavenly level—at least to the level of the fourth-dimensional Astral Realm*. That is why the principle of spiritual possession exists. If devils and evil spirits could enter maternal wombs and reincarnate, many more devils would be born into this world. If this would be the case, this world would be much more hopeless.

---

* TF: The other world, or the spirit world, is divided into different levels according to the inhabitants' state of mind and the level of enlightenment. The Earth's spirit world extends from the fourth dimension to the ninth. The Astral Realm is located in the fourth dimension, and those who still retain an earthly lifestyle but who are aware of themselves as spiritual beings inhabit there. The fourth dimension also has an area called hell. Refer to *The Nine Dimensions* (New York: IRH Press, 2012), *Spiritual World 101* (Tokyo: HS Press, 2015), and *My Journey through the Spirit World* (New York: IRH Press, 2018).

The spiritual influence behind some criminal cases

Since hell is located very close to this world, people on earth are spiritually influenced by hell. If your mind is attuned to a spirit in hell, that spirit can possess you and get a taste of life on earth.

There are cases where people with mental disorders commit crimes without remembering what they did. This type of criminal has no memory of the moment of stabbing someone, for example. At that time, the person's soul most probably leaves the physical body and an evil spirit takes its place. The evil spirit then stabs the victim and leaves, and when the person regains consciousness, he or she has no memory of committing the crime.

Such criminal cases are tried in courts under secular judicial systems, but judgment is quite difficult because these cases involve spiritual possession. The penal laws can certainly exempt or reduce sentences in cases where criminals are considered unable to assume responsibility for their actions: that is, mentally unable to control themselves. Doctors' diagnoses and other professional assessments are taken into consideration for the court decision, so these types of exceptional cases are somewhat recognized by society. But it is a little difficult to prove these cases from a religious perspective, and these types of crimes are very tough to judge.

The difficulty of judging people Under spiritual influence

Whether people who are under spiritual influence can live a good life is determined by the people around them. For this reason, it is very difficult to evaluate them as good or bad. If those around them say they are odd, they could be labeled as such, but if people who believe in spiritual matters surround them, they could receive support.

When I first started Happy Science, I created a membership application system and maintained the system for three years. Those who wanted to join Happy Science had to submit an application form, and I would personally judge whether to accept them. I remember one of the applications was from a person who had graduated from the University of Tokyo, Faculty of Law, some years earlier than I did but was confined in a mental hospital at the time. According to what he wrote, he was married and had a job, but after he started to hear the voices of spirits and experience various spiritual phenomena, he was thought to be mentally ill by his family and was admitted to a mental hospital. He asked me to help him get out of the hospital.

He may have seen me as a person sharing some similarity, but graduating from the same university has no meaning in such spiritual matters. In this sense, judging whether one is sane or insane is extremely difficult for people connected to that person. When a person is under strong spiritual influence, their actions might show many eccentricities. It is a matter of how to view those actions, either as too erratic or within reason, from an empirical perspective.

4

Exorcism 1:
Drastic Measures that Come with Risk

Scary cases of the Vatican-style exorcism

It is true that people under the influence of evil spirits act violently and make strange sounds, as portrayed in exorcism-related movies. Sometimes they may inflict self-injury and hurt themselves so badly that they bleed. The more frightening case is when they assault others by hitting, kicking, or swinging a baseball bat. It is dangerous when they start causing injuries to others.

Once they reach a point where they entirely lose control of themselves, those around them must take measures to defend themselves. The solution is either to use medication such as sedatives to keep them calm or to ask for an exorcism to be performed on them. The latter is possible if there is objective evidence and the Vatican grants permission, though it seems increasingly difficult to receive permission nowadays. But exorcism can sometimes trigger a harsh situation where violence is involved.

As a law student, I studied the following court case. When a priest performed an exorcism, the patient started to act violently. So the priest also resorted to violence, which eventually led to the death of the patient. The point was how the court judged the case in relation to the priest practicing his freedom of religion. In this case, the priest was found guilty based on the idea that even though the act of dispelling evil spirits could be considered a part of religious belief, it was too extreme because it resulted in the death of the patient.

In this sense, performing an exorcism could be quite difficult because the patient could become violent and begin to attack the exorcist, and at times become like a savage animal. So, there may well be times when the exorcist must use force to subdue the patient. Mental hospitals, for example, often bind the patients' limbs or tie their bodies down because otherwise, the patients could exert extremely strong power. Some of the Vatican-style exorcism movies also have scenes in which the possessed person is bound using leather straps, and that is because the possessed can sometimes demonstrate extraordinary power.

In the case of devils speaking in tongues

Devils in the Western countries have strong psychokinetic power, so they can probably demonstrate a strong physical force. Movies of exorcism have scenes in which the possessed person floats in the air, clings to the ceiling, or crawls across a wall. I have not witnessed such cases in real life, so I am not sure if it is really possible. The world is vast, so these things might happen in certain places, but I have never seen anyone moving across the ceiling defying gravity, crawling like a gecko, or crawling down the stairs facing upward.

It is possible for possessed people to hurt their own bodies, try to grab other people, use abusive words, or speak in tongues—meaning they speak a language they do not know. When people speak in a language unknown to them, it can be the Holy Spirit speaking through them, but it can also be a devil. Sometimes the possessed person speaks Latin, but even in that case devils could be involved. Those who worked as clergymen, including priests and monks, from Roman times to the Middle Ages, could read Latin, and they would read the Bible out loud in Latin when performing an exorcism. And in some cases, devils can also speak in Latin.

There is an ancient language called Aramaic, which Jesus is said to have spoken. Many of his disciples were fishermen from the regions around the Sea of Galilee, and they used Aramaic. This language was used in the region of the birthplace of Jesus, and it is said that Jesus usually gave his sermon in Aramaic. I, too, can speak Aramaic.

In some cases, when someone speaks in tongues, it is often reported that they use Aramaic. Such phenomena can occur.

There are also cases in which someone speaks a much older language, such as the ones used in ancient Mesopotamia or Egypt. Again, it could be the Holy Spirit speaking through the person; but if not, a powerful devil, rather than a normal evil spirit, is at work, given that it has a good command of such an old language. The devil could have once been a high-ranking priest, king, or dignitary who was a close adviser to a king, and now holds great power in hell. It can often be the case that such a spirit is in possession of someone. To fight such spirits, the Bible, cross, and holy water seem to be insufficient. It seems to be quite difficult to fight such evil spirits.

Exorcism 2:
Defensive Measures with
Gradual Effects

*A way to safeguard yourself against constant attacks
From evil spirits and devils*

The above method is like an operation done under emergency conditions, but since there are more chances of accidents, I would recommend a defensive way that gradually takes effect like herbal medicine. That is to say, take precautionary measures every day. Any recommendation to lead a moral life may sound silly nowadays, and in this sense, religions may also be ridiculed. However, to safeguard yourself against the constant attack from evil spirits and devils, it is essential to maintain a well-regulated life based on the right faith. Work and study in the right manner, and make sure to keep your life in order.

People today may probably find many of the Buddhist precepts too demanding. There are precepts that deny, for example, the desire for money or the opposite sex. There are also ones that prohibit lying, drinking alcohol, and killing or harming other people. Some even extend to the prohibition of killing animals. For this reason, people may find it difficult to strictly abide by some of these rules in the modern day. Nevertheless, it is true that these rules have a certain benefit. They warn people that life is full of traps that could lead people to destroying their characters and their lives.

The danger of impairment of reasoning Caused by alcohol and drugs

One of the ancient precepts prohibits drinking alcohol, but in the modern context, it should also include bans on excessive smoking, narcotics, stimulants, and other drugs. While Japan is still strict regarding drugs, the U.S. seems to have taken a somewhat permissive stance; even a person who once served as the President of the U.S. has admitted his past experience of using marijuana, and there is a general trend to approve the use of drugs. While drugs have the effect of numbing one's reasoning ability and creating temporary pleasure, they can sometimes be quite dangerous. The temporary impairment of reasoning will only make people vulnerable to evil possession.

In bars, for example, many troublesome spirits or spirits of villains are lingering around, and if you drink too much, you can be possessed by one of them. For this reason, it would be wise to set rules for yourself to not excessively drink alcohol and not staying out too late.

If people drink so much that they lose their awareness, their personality could completely change and those around them would not know who is really talking. Some might become extremely drunk and wander about the streets at night like vagabonds, whereas others would nonsensically yell out in a park or lose consciousness on a bench at a train station. These people have definitely lost the power of reasoning, and it is highly likely that they have been taken over by an evil spirit. When people are highly intoxicated, they lose control of themselves, so it becomes extremely easy for evil spirits to possess them.

In the past, while I was still working for a trading company, there were times I had to go out for drinks after work to socialize with co-workers. I learned from those experiences that even though high spirits would normally come when I called for them, after I consumed some alcohol, they did not always appear, and if they did, I could not identify which spirit it was. From this I can say that it is highly dangerous to conduct spiritual phenomena such as receiving spiritual messages after consuming an excessive amount of alcohol.

The same is probably true with drugs, such as narcotics and stimulants. With the use of these drugs, people might artificially create a state similar to that experienced by a spiritual medium. In India, for instance, there are many drug users among yogis; in this way, they may have a psychedelic experience called a "trip." This may include an actual trip to the spirit world in the form of an out-of-body experience or hearing of the spirits' voices. Such an experience should essentially be achieved through the practice of Zen meditation, but since meditation takes effort and drugs can be purchased, people resort to the easy way to have a similar experience. However, it is not a truly trusted way. This is a difficult issue because ancient religions are often involved in this matter. Even so, correcting one's lifestyle is essential.

Know your "unguarded areas" and Try to solve your problems

When evil spirits or devils target a family, they are always searching for a weak point, and once they discover it, they will surely attack this weak point. When wolves target sheep, for example, they will try for a lamb, an injured member, or a stray that has wandered from the flock. In the same way, it is easy to target the loners who failed to adapt to the culture of an organization or those who do not fit in well with their families.

Therefore, evil spirits enter through back doors and attack the easiest targets, just like the burglars that sneak into a house. Burglars can find an unguarded spot by observing the house. They may see, for instance, that a window can be easily broken or that the back door provides easy entry. They may even find out that a spare key is always hidden in the mailbox or under some potted plants. They can easily break into a house in this way. There are many such cases of burglary.

If I were to compare the human body to a house, initially, a window might be broken, then a door, and then the pillars. A wall could then crumble or a hole could open up in the roof. In this way, there can be many unguarded areas.

The Japanese folktale, *Hoichi the Earless*, is the story of a man named Hoichi who, by the help of a monk, had a Buddhist sutra written all over his body to protect himself against a malicious spirit from the Heike Clan. But because the monk forgot to write on his ears, his ears were torn away by the spirit. This story shows how evil spirits and devils usually target an unguarded area.

In the course of life, people inevitably have worries and troubles. If you want to know what your worry or "unguarded area" is, just think about what you are repeatedly thinking about during the day when you are not particularly doing anything. That is most probably what you are concerned about the most or is a problem you are unable to solve. What frequently occupies your mind is mostly the source of your worry. If an evil spirit or devil discovers your concern, it will enter your mind through it. For this reason, it is important to solve problems that can be solved by worldly means and prevent unguarded areas from forming in a worldly sense. I recommend that you make an effort to remove such unguarded areas one by one.

Do not blame others or the environment, but Strive to increase your ability to judge good and bad

When you cannot solve a problem yourself, you could seek advice from someone with more insight or more experience than you and follow their advice. That is a possible way out.

Those who are easily possessed by evil spirits are usually indecisive, and these people are easily swayed by the opinions of others. That is why they are easily controlled by the whispers of evil spirits. In that sense, it is important to make a conscious effort to develop the ability to judge what is right and wrong by accumulating knowledge and experience and using the grit or the strength of your entire soul. Then you will be less likely to be targeted by evil spirits.

If you lack this ability, you will be unable to solve problems that can normally be easily solved; instead, you will amplify these problems until they become serious matters. There are people with limited practical skills, people who are indecisive, and people who cannot distinguish important matters from trifling matters and prioritize correctly. When these people are tasked with responsibilities beyond their capabilities, they will no longer be able to make sound judgments and will start making mistakes. This will create "unguarded areas."

If these people are criticized or belittled at such times, they will feel hurt and become unable to think of anything but those negative remarks. Their minds will be filled with hatred. In general, small-minded people cannot accept responsibility for what has happened, and they always blame others or external circumstances. They blame, for example, their parents, siblings, teachers at school, or superiors or colleagues at work. Of course, we cannot say that these people around them had completely nothing to do with the matter; they may have been at fault to some extent, or it could have been caused by environmental factors. However, as I have repeatedly taught, it is fundamentally important to first reflect on yourself and then take a step forward by doing what you can do.

Help from others is indeed appreciated, but it is easier for others and the spirits in heaven to help those who are making an effort to solve the problem on their own. This is noteworthy. You may complain, for instance, that you are unhappy because your father was laid off from work, or that things are terrible now because your mother has a bad character, or your family's fate worsened because your grandfather caused a traffic accident. Perhaps you were bullied by a cruel class leader and were unable to attend school. There are different reasons why people suffer misfortune, but in the end, those who are more inclined to stand on their own two feet and start afresh have higher chances to attain salvation.

Humility will provide protection

People with some degree of spiritual ability will sometimes be confronted by evil spirits. At such times, they need to be careful not to become conceited. They might certainly defeat weaker spirits, but as they continually engage in dispelling evil spirits, they will eventually be challenged by a stronger spirit that is beyond their power. There is definitely a limit to what they can handle, and at some point, a spirit will appear with a stronger power than theirs. If, at such a time, they are conceited, take too much pride in themselves, or believe themselves to be some great deity, Buddha, or high spirit, they will fail to recognize that they have already fallen victim to the devil. They must be careful about this point.

I teach the importance of staying humble not just because it is a good virtue. By maintaining humility at all times, you can also protect yourself. So please maintain this virtue. It is similar to crawling on your belly in a battlefield; if you keep your head low and inch forward on your stomach, you can avoid bullets. In the same way, by maintaining a humble attitude, you will be less likely to be hit by the enemy's bullets.

On the other hand, those who are quick to become conceited or arrogant, or boast about their achievements or abilities over drinks can easily be "shot down." They are the type of people that cannot objectively see themselves, and they are easy targets. Like in hunting, animals that stand up straight and do not move are easy targets and will therefore be the first to be shot. Thus, I recommend that you advance with caution and prudence.

6

Through Faith, Become One with God

The power to ultimately win against strong devils

Quelling devils is not easy. Even if at first you may think you can expel a devil, stronger ones will gradually emerge. This may not be a well-known fact because not many people have experienced this kind of process, but you will eventually lose if you do not have faith. Please know this.

It would be wrong to assume you can win with your ability alone. Some may actually witness various spiritual phenomena before their very eyes and believe they have some psychic power. But in the end, without strong faith in God or Buddha, you cannot fully defend yourself. You must be one with God or Buddha. You are mistaken to assume that you can fight alone and be victorious. The Japanese swordmaster Musashi Miyamoto fought dozens of enemies with just a sword, but that is not how things usually work.

Take, for example, the movie *Constantine*. I am not sure if it can be classified as a horror film, but the story involves the spirit world. Keanu Reeves, the actor who starred in *Little Buddha*, played the main character in

Constantine. In the movie, the protagonist has lung cancer due to heavy smoking. He undergoes many experiences, including his cancer being removed by the devil and his soul leaving his body to travel to the other world. But considering the character of the protagonist, it is normally very difficult for such a person to protect himself from a devil.

Spiritual ability is an innate quality to some extent, but even if one has it, it is important to maintain an attitude of discipline while safeguarding oneself in this world. The former professional baseball player Ichiro, for example, would give off an unassailable, fierce air once in the batter's box. A religious practitioner essentially must have such a solemn atmosphere and should not have unguarded areas.

People do have desires as long as they live as humans. They may want money, status, power that comes with the status, or fame. Where money, status, and power are concerned, there will always be the opposite sex, and the desire to own the opposite sex will also arise. As long as these desires remain within reasonable limits, they can be permitted to a certain extent. For instance, an American president marrying a supermodel is a private decision. People can only wish him good luck. It may have a positive effect on an election. However, if you become too greedy and desire many things beyond what you deserve, you will most likely fail.

The importance of building up small successes

I often talk about the importance of starting from the ordinary and steadily building up small successes, but this is not a recommendation to be mediocre. Sometimes you may be lucky enough to hit a grand slam home run, but if you always aim for great success, you will get into the habit of swinging for the fences even though home runs are not a common occurrence. After tasting a huge success once, people will hardly forget it.

In Japan, a book was published on what became of the lottery winners who won ¥100 million (about US$1 million). In most cases, the end results were not very good. While winning small amounts in a lottery or drawing small prizes would not make much of a difference, receiving an unexpectedly large sum of money that is beyond one's ability to manage it often accompanies a higher risk of downfall.

I once saw a series of massive advertisements for a local noodle shop in a nationally circulated newspaper and wondered how it was possible for the noodle shop owner to do so. Then, a rumor followed that the owner had won a lottery jackpot, which enabled him to put out large advertisements; I am not sure if the rumor was true or not. Things may work well while the money lasts and his business runs smoothly, but if his business slows down and he runs out of money, he may well have to face a harsh reality. If he has gotten used to such an extravagant business style, it may be extremely difficult for him to cut back his expenses.

At the Japan National High School Baseball Tournament, a team that wins a great victory with more than twenty runs or more than a ten-run lead tends to lose the next game. That is probably because the players lose focus after the overwhelming victory. Even if they are told to stay focused, they naturally loosen up. We need to be careful of such a tendency.

The sixteenth-century Japanese feudal lord Shingen Takeda said that one should be content with a 60 percent victory. That is because victory can cause the victors to create unguarded areas. Losses can certainly create weaknesses; one may feel insignificant and resentful, may become timid and lose motivation for battle, or may develop the habit of making excuses. But victories can also cause weaknesses.

In that sense, it is important to build up concrete efforts rather than aim for a quick and easy success. It is better to make steady efforts so that people around you would agree that you deserve any success that comes with it. This is why I recommend that you build up small successes. Sometimes, an unexpectedly big success can bring about a perfect life, but this rarely happens; it is like seeking a rare salvation with a one-in-a-thousand or one-in-ten-thousand chance. In most cases, things will not go that well. So please accumulate steady efforts.

Love can sometimes create unguarded areas In one's mind

Young people, in particular, often experience failure in relationships with the opposite sex. But after people pass a certain age, their way of thinking changes. They will become able to view things from the perspective of the overall balance of life. For instance, they develop the abilities to judge the importance of work, the weight of responsibility, or the best distance to maintain good relationships with others. Once they have gained such abilities, they have some understanding of how to maintain an appropriate distance or deepen their relationships with the opposite sex as well. They also begin to understand that making too many empty promises will later cause them serious troubles.

As you develop the skills at work, you will deepen the ability to build sound relationships with the opposite sex. However, when you are young, this is not often the case. As in *Romeo and Juliet*, sometimes young people may find everything to be a matter of "life or death," leading them to the decision of leaving their job and running away with their lover. They may find themselves forced into a corner in this way.

Being young means being full of dreams and possibilities, but no matter how intelligent one is, there is unfortunately a limit to wisdom. While still young, you cannot understand how differently you might view things in ten or twenty years when you have more experience. Know that imprudence is inevitable in youth no matter how smart a person may be.

People who have gained rich experience from many decades of life can see dangerous tendencies in others even if they are not necessarily intelligent in a worldly sense. That is because they have observed many things, including the rise and fall of different people. Even if their education ended at middle school, they can see potential failure in others and point out, for example, that a person will get in trouble with women, alcohol, gambling, or fraud at work. They can see, to some extent, the dangerous tendencies of others. It is worth noting that standardized test scores do not necessarily determine one's true cleverness. It is essential to observe people's true natures.

Love, in particular, can create unguarded areas that could be easy targets for devils to attack, depending on how it is expressed. This is taught both in Buddhism and Christianity. It is also true that as long as we live on earth, we cannot completely escape the matter of love. Having a good balance is very difficult. To avoid getting caught up in the "trap" of love, some may choose to live alone by totally rejecting it. Monks and priests may live that way. Even so, many unexpected mistakes seem to endlessly occur.

In modern society, people tend to understand that love means to be loved by someone. Certainly, this feeling should not be flatly denied because being loved by others means being supported by them. When you love someone, your sense of attachment to that person can become the target of devils to attack; but, at the same time, your love can also serve to protect that person. In that case, devils cannot easily bring that person down.

Love includes the feelings between a particular man and woman, but there are also people who are loved by a large number of people, regardless of gender. When you are loved by many people, it also means you are receiving much support, just like a pole that stands upright supported by many ropes, and you can hardly be toppled. It is not very easy to defeat a person who is genuinely loved by others.

On the other hand, there is very shallow love: a very narrow, modern, contract-based love. In the case of such love, people can easily argue over the validity of the contract or whether to break it or not. In the end, the negative consequence of the relationship would be a bigger issue than whether there was love or not. That is why Shakyamuni Buddha taught that one should not have loved ones.

Those who do not practice teachings Cannot be protected

When advancing on the path to enlightenment, it is difficult to maintain a romantic relationship; it often becomes an obstacle. In that sense, Shakyamuni Buddha had a somewhat detached attitude, as seen in the Agon Sutra that is supposedly based on what Buddha had actually said.

One example of Buddha's detached attitude is seen in the analogy of pointing at the moon. Buddha taught that while he could point at the moon, it was up to each individual to actually look at the moon; it is not possible to force someone and the person needs to see it with his or her own eyes. By this, Buddha meant that while he could teach people the direction in which they should aim for in their enlightenment, spiritual discipline, and the study of the Truth, it is up to each individual to practice.

This means that those who practice his teachings will be saved, whereas those who do not practice will not be saved. Shakyamuni Buddha was fairly realistic; his words were based on his experience of observing both the people who could be saved and the people who could not. The Buddhist monk Kobo-Daishi Kukai also had such a realistic outlook. I have an impression that he viewed the world quite coolly.

In the past, I watched the Japanese TV drama *Onmyoji* (literally, "Yin-Yang Master") featuring the character of Abe-no-Seimei. Abe-no-Seimei, played by Goro Inagaki, was portrayed as having a Buddhist-like realistic attitude. One of his lines was, "Whether or not a person possessed by a vengeful spirit can be saved ultimately depends on that person."

A man could be saved if he became aware that the woman he loved has turned into a vengeful spirit and now possesses him. Then, he would be able to regain his true consciousness and take back control of his will. But he would not be saved if he clung on to his former lover without realizing that she has become a horrible demon. If he still loved her after she became what appeared to be a demon reduced to skin and bones to the objective eye, then nothing could be done; it was up to him whether to be saved or not. This was pointed out in the drama; it was very much influenced by the Buddhist way of thinking.

Even if people listen to my teachings in a similar way, some people can be saved while others will spin off and cannot be saved. In some sense, this cannot be helped.

I give teachings. If you practice them, you can protect yourself. But those who are not willing to practice them will not be protected.

For this reason, if you feel, "I'm the best," you will eventually fail. Without faith, you cannot protect yourself in the end. With small ups and downs—experiencing success at times and failure at other times—your mind can be swayed, allowing a devil to enter such unguarded areas. This concludes my talk centering on the basic knowledge of how to become a real exorcist.

Chapter Four

Exorcists as Religious Professionals

Q&A Session on "The Real Exorcist"

Given on May 9, 2018
at Special Lecture Hall, Happy Science, Tokyo, Japan

How to Check One's Faith

Questioner A

We learned from the previous lecture that we need to have faith to ultimately defeat devils, but I'm afraid that even if we believe we are faithful, sometimes we unknowingly allow evil to enter our minds. Please tell us how to check if our faith has deviated from the right path.

Small mistakes would not be allowed When one's social position rises

Ryuho Okawa

This is a difficult issue. It may not only apply to religion. For example, if you are promoted at work, your way of decision making and attitude toward other people should change. The same is true when your influence over others becomes greater through work.

In the world of entertainment, a new talent can gradually gain popularity and eventually become a national or even an international star. The higher their status rises, the more they will be treated like a politician or the CEO of a large company. Even in the entertainment industry, some people will actually receive medals. Honors are awarded according to how much influence or contribution they have made on society. This is true in any industry; company executives, scholars, singers, or actors can be awarded. One's social position can change in this way, so first you need to be aware of this.

Your question is about how to check your level of faith when you believe you are faithful, but in religion too, there is the issue of your position in the religious organization. If you are in a higher position, you will have more influence on a large number of people, so any mistaken remark you make might cause trouble to many.

The same is true when you are involved in acts of salvation. When you are in a low position and your power of exorcism is not expected to be high, your mistake or failure will not develop into a serious problem. However, as your position gets higher and people have high expectations from you, a mistake that might have been overlooked in a lower position could develop into a serious problem.

For example, it would be a problem if someone with the qualification of a Happy Science headquarters lecturer did not know "El Cantare Fight"* or did not read

---

* TF: A spiritual rite of Happy Science to exorcise evil spirits and devils. See Chapter One for details.

The Laws of the Sun. Lower-level staff could be excused or would only receive a reprimand, but this would not be the case for staff in higher positions.

In higher positions, those filled with self-love will receive disapproval. It is natural for people to earnestly seek approval from others in the beginning. Babies constantly seek their parents' attention, expressing hunger or the urge to pee or poo. They want milk and crave many other things. However, as you grow into an adult, you must develop the strength to control and restrain the desires, and when in a position above others, you must refrain from insisting on your own benefit and instead put more effort into helping others. The youth naturally think about their own progress, but as they achieve higher positions, they have to consider how to help others grow and develop.

The required level of faith will also change With the rise in one's position

Similar to how your way of thinking will change with a rise in position, the required level of faith will become higher. In the beginning, your faith would be considered sufficient if it served to protect you, but once your status or position advances, such a level would no longer be adequate.

For example, a lay member who does not actively participate in religious activities may prefer not to reveal their Happy Science membership at their workplace, worrying that disclosing this may cause some negative reaction among colleagues. When religious issues pop up in a chat over a drink, that person might not argue against negative remarks on religion. However, when it comes to the lay members who have some specific responsibility in the group and the staff members who assume positions of branch managers or higher, things are a little different. If these people criticize Happy Science teachings, its executives, or its founder, they may have no choice but to leave the group because such negative remarks would go against their interests.

The same can be said of a company employee. You cannot directly speak badly of the president of the company you work for, nor can you openly make remarks that would go against the company's policies. If you did, you would not be able to remain in the company. This may also be connected to a matter of mature behavior.

In essence, one should not boast about his or her level of faith. Jesus Christ also restricted this behavior. Jesus would often say that when you pray, you should not be seen by others and that you should pray calmly, all alone, in secret. Some people try to show how faithful they are, but their display of devotion will create unguarded areas in their minds for vanity to slip in. That is why Jesus taught that one should pray by oneself in a quiet place. In any case, your faith would be tested to see how truthful it is.

Faith has real power

Faith is based on the depth of one's knowledge of the Truth and on the strong will to seek enlightenment. In other words, faith is based on one's desire to be closer to God or Buddha. By having faith, believers are protecting religious leaders beyond the level of just supporting and helping them. With the love of God or Buddha, these religious leaders work on earth as His representative. These representatives of God or Buddha are constantly attacked by the spirits of both the living and the dead as well as by various things of this world, so they are actually protected by the faith of many people. This is a very important point.

In this sense, too, I believe Japanese people are lax in their ideas about religion. When they go to religious countries and say they are atheists or do not believe in any religion, they are sometimes misunderstood and considered less than human or at the level of animals. Since the end of the Meiji Era, Japan has created a strange culture where people without faith are regarded as more intellectual, and this tendency became especially strong after World War II. Such a culture is indeed embarrassing, and we need to create an opposite sense of values.

To do so, we need to create a rightful religion, one that society can accept to a certain extent. If there are many misguided religious groups, it would be difficult for religion to be highly regarded. A reform movement must arise from inside the circle of religion.

While loyalty is necessary for companies, faith is a much more serious matter. Faith has real power, and it truly works.

Faith is of course your feelings toward the holy Gohonzon (the object of worship), the founder and leader who originally created the religious group. But at the same time, faith is indispensable in order for you to receive spiritual energy and become one with God or Buddha when fighting against evil spirits and devils. Without faith, your fight will be reduced to your own individual battle, and you will eventually lose if any powerful enemies appear.

You may sometimes have to deal with a person under negative spiritual influence, but if that person is possessed by five or six spirits, it will not be easy to dispel them all; it will be beyond an individual's power. If someone is possessed by the spirit of his or her father who died in an accident, that person can send the father's spirit back to heaven by taking part in Happy Science seminars or conducting a memorial service for the deceased father. However, it is hard to dispel five or six spirits that take turns in possessing a person for decades due to his or her mistaken thoughts. When dealing with such a person, you need to be connected to the central God or Buddha through Happy Science faith; otherwise, you will also be in danger. Please know this.

Worldly value systems must not be brought Into the world of religion

One thing you need to bear in mind at such times is that you should not bring worldly value systems into the world of religion. This is where people often make a mistake.

Some believers might judge a manager of a local temple, a head minister, or a lecturer of a shoja from a worldly perspective by thinking, "I graduated from a top-ranking university and work at a top-tier company; but the head minister of this shoja is a graduate of a third-rate university, so his prayers must not be very powerful." If the person has this kind of thinking, the spirit possessing him will not be dispelled.

In Buddhism, Shakyamuni Buddha did away with the caste system in his group, and monks were not judged based on the caste they originally belonged to. One's position in the group was generally decided on the basis of how long one had been a monk. In addition, when a monk attained a certain level of enlightenment and became an arhat, it meant the monk became closer to the master. So, that monk was given a special position. The followers belonged to different castes, such as the Brahmins, Kshatriyas, Vaishyas, and Shudras, but upon becoming monks, those worldly castes were discarded.

Jealousy and a sense of rivalry Seen in Christ's disciples

Jesus treated his followers with the same spirit. Hardly any of his disciples had high social standing. They included fishermen, a tax collector, and the brother of Jesus, whose own father was a carpenter. A carpenter would be equivalent to a construction worker in today's society.

In fact, Judas was the most educated of Jesus' twelve disciples. He is said to have studied at a proper Jewish school when he was young. In Jesus' group, he was the treasurer, so he had both "money" and "education." Such a person eventually betrayed Jesus. He was probably conceited, being the only one who received proper Jewish education and who was qualified as a rabbi, a teacher. That is why he was approached by some of the Roman rulers and by the Jewish priests who had sold their souls to the Romans and was enticed into betraying his master for a small amount of money.

Later, Judas regretted his betrayal of his master and hung himself. He had sold his master for thirty pieces of silver—perhaps the equivalent of US$300-US$3,000 in today's currency. Some favorable accounts say that Judas hoped to witness a miracle to save Jesus.

As mentioned, Judas was the treasurer of the group; he handled and managed the group's money, but it seemed that the group was always having financial problems. Despite that, female believers would treat Jesus lavishly.

Among the followers was a woman named Mary, who on one occasion poured scented oil onto Jesus' feet and wiped it off with her hair. The oil Mary used cost three hundred denarii; it is said to have been equivalent to a year's worth of wages, about US$30,000 in today's currency. Judas viewed it as a waste and accused her by saying, "Why was this fragrant oil not sold for three hundred denarii and given to the poor?" He thought that such an amount of money could have helped support the group for about a year.

But Jesus replied, "Leave her alone" and "For you always have the poor with you, but you will not always have me." Being aware that his departure from this world was nearing, he approved of Mary's actions as an expression of her faith and her highest respect for him. He understood that she tried to do her utmost to serve him, which would be remembered as a historic event. While Judas rationally saw it as a waste to use the costly scented oil to clean feet, Jesus judged it to be a proper action because his death was nearing and her action would be remembered for two thousand years to come.

There is also the story of Mary and her sister Martha. While Martha was busy preparing dinner for Jesus and his disciples, Mary just sat listening at Jesus' feet. Martha was upset with her sister and told her to help out in the kitchen, for which Jesus gently scolded her.

From a worldly, commonsensical point of view, Judas and Martha's assertions sound reasonable, but from a religious perspective, they certainly seemed to have had jealousy and a sense of rivalry that are typical of humans. Values in the world of faith are somewhat different from those of this world, and it is wrong to consider what is valued in this world to be equally important in religion. Conversely, sometimes that which has no value in this world can have great value in religion. I hope you will understand this point.

The difficulty of having a pure heart
In the world of religion

There are many things that are considered valuable in this world, such as social standing, fame, power, and money. They are indeed useful. However, there are also times when they are not.

For example, donating money to a religion does not necessarily guarantee an immediate breakoff from evil spirits. Some people may believe that a large donation would make a priest conduct an exorcism with more seriousness and that the possessing evil spirit would surely be expelled. This can sometimes happen. The heart of charity or offering is indeed precious. Even so, the power of a religious exorcism depends on the degree of spiritual discipline and faith of those involved. In this sense, the idea that the donation amount makes a difference over the power of exorcism is a misguided way of thinking and we should separate the two factors.

It is essential not to apply worldly values to the world of faith. We need to be determined not to do so; otherwise, we would be inevitably inclined to uphold worldly ideas. The issue of age is one such example. Some disciples may hesitate to open their hearts to the advice of a younger master. Another example is gender. Some may hesitate to seek advice because it's a she or he. Others may feel proud that they are more good-looking than the master.

There are also people who boast about the duration of their spiritual training. Before joining Happy Science, some may have trained themselves by meditating under a waterfall for ten years, engaged in ascetic training in the mountains, or completed a thousand-day pilgrimage of shrines, and their achievements may have been honored and reported in newspapers. These people may feel proud of themselves and believe they are different from other believers. Yet things are not so simple.

Although all people are evaluated differently in this world, once they have entered the world of faith, they need to cast away all worldly reputation. Otherwise, it is difficult to have a pure mind. It is important to know this.

There are certainly differences in one's position in an organization, but job positions are sometimes given as an expedient means to run things smoothly. In Happy Science, too, positions in the group can only be temporary and the true greatness of a person does not necessarily accord with their worldly status. Each and every person needs to have the attitude of a practitioner of the Truth.

You cannot protect yourself
Without an established faith

Faith should not be used as a tool to achieve something or to show off. Unless you perceive faith as real power, you can neither protect yourself nor save other people. Therefore, it is important to know that there is a limit to one's own spiritual ability. Only when you have established your faith will you be able to continuously protect yourself and also save other people. I hope this is clearly understood.

Certainly, miracles can happen when you, as a Happy Science lecturer, conduct a *kigan* (ritual prayer) at a shoja. But miracles occur because the entire organization has created a spiritual field and a system of faith to save people. So it is wrong to believe that you can still make miracles on your own even if you leave Happy Science. Such a thought will easily allow a devil to enter your mind and manipulate you. Please do not misunderstand this point.

Spiritual messages conducted by Happy Science Have gained social credibility

There was a case where a former Happy Science believer enticed some of our believers into her group, boasting that she could receive spiritual messages. She was an active member but left Happy Science in 1994, the year I stopped recording spiritual messages and started to base our activities on my teachings. Later, she started publishing what she claimed to be "spiritual messages" and formed her own group. She insisted that she could converse with spirits while Ryuho Okawa had lost his spiritual abilities.

I knew nothing of this because I did not see any of her books advertised in newspapers. So I was surprised when I heard that she had lured about twenty believers away from one of our local branches with the false claim that I had lost my spiritual abilities. Then I heard that her books were displayed on the bottom shelf of a large bookstore.

After I learned that she had influenced our believers with such a claim, I decided to restart publishing spiritual messages; I have now published more than five hundred books (as of April 2019).* I thus demonstrated how I was still capable of publishing any number of books of spiritual messages. My spiritual messages are like "bombs." When I published them in rapid succession, they were like the bombing of a Boeing B-29, and her logic rapidly crumbled.

While newspapers have not advertised her books, they have advertised mine. This may sound strange, but it shows the difference in the level of social credibility. The truth is that people with sound opinions understand the messages I have published over the last thirty years, and they judge them as quite sensible and different from others. For example, *Sankei Shimbun* and *Yomiuri Shimbun* newspapers had large advertisements of our spiritual message of the late author Ryotaro Shiba,

---

* TF: The spiritual messages cover various topics, including religion, politics, economics, education, science, and entertainment. The spirits are of historical figures and guardian spirits of living people.

in which his spirit gives his thoughts on patriotism. *Sankei Shimbun* also advertised our book of spiritual messages of the guardian spirits of Moon Jae-in and Kim Jong-un as well as those of the late cultural critic Shoichi Watanabe.

These companies understand very well what it means to advertise the spiritual messages of Ryotaro Shiba and Shoichi Watanabe in their newspapers. Mr. Ryotaro Shiba was previously a journalist at the Sankei Shimbun, and after leaving Sankei and becoming an author, his novels were serialized in *Sankei Shimbun*. A large advertisement of his spiritual message in the newspaper would be equivalent to one of his editorials appearing in the newspaper. I assume his opinions were fairly close to the policies of the company. That is why they approved of the advertisement of the book.

Mr. Shoichi Watanabe had passed away just a year before we advertised his spiritual message books, so there was an apparent risk for the newspaper company. There are many self-proclaimed psychic mediums. In Japan, it is said that there are over ten thousand such people. If all of them claimed to have received spiritual messages from Mr. Shoichi Watanabe and Mr. Ryotaro Shiba and published them as books, the public would be confused and there would be many problems.

Such spirits do not appear just anywhere because they too have pride. I suppose they choose an appropriate and reliable outlet for their spiritual messages. They would be seen questionable if they appeared in many places. Some people may claim that the spirit of Mr. Shoichi Watanabe should appear to a Catholic medium because he was Catholic. In reality, it would be impossible for a Catholic organization to publish a spiritual message because it would be considered heretical and the writer would possibly face the risk of excommunication. Such a difference in perspectives exists in religion. In any case, social credibility is essential, and it is important that one is trusted as a religious person.

How to Maintain A Good State of Mind

Questioner B

I have heard that some people have difficulty overcoming spiritual disturbance. When they take a kigan to exorcise evil spirits, they repent their mistakes and regain their faith and devotion to God. At that time, they receive light from heaven and appear to recover. But it is only temporary; they soon start to waver in their minds and again come under spiritual possession. They seem to repeat this experience. I would like to hear your advice for these people on how to maintain a good spiritual condition and stabilize their minds.

The law of inertia works for mental states

Ryuho Okawa

Such a fluctuation is a typical trait of ordinary people, and it cannot be helped. They may repent their mistakes when they sense holiness in a solemn atmosphere, but after returning to everyday activities, they shift back to their former state. This is the usual pattern of ordinary people; it is generally what happens.

Even so, it is an exceptional experience for them to be moved to tears and regain their faith when they participate in a kigan ceremony or other rituals in places such as Happy Science shoja. It is better than having no such spiritual experience. However, those feelings eventually fade away at home or in the workplace; as they go on with their daily lives, they are gradually dragged into a material sense of values.

This is the law of inertia. People take a certain course during their years of life on earth, and they cannot change direction all of a sudden even if they want to. As physics shows, a train will keep moving forward even after the brakes are applied, as will a car. Because of this law of inertia, things cannot stop all of a sudden, or with just one attempt.

One can certainly experience a change of heart from a little advice or by taking part in a ritual. Whether the change is only temporary and one returns to the former state of mind depends on how long or the degree to which the person has lived in the wrong way. It depends on the flow of their lifestyle that has continued from the past.

For people who have more or less lived in a way that accords with faith in the past, it is relatively easy to change their ways when they are deeply moved by a spiritual experience and are determined to alter their way of thinking. However, it would be difficult for people who have acted in ways that are opposite to faith in the past or have been surrounded by people who do not believe in spiritual matters. Even if they happen to see or hear their guardian spirits or feel light when a priest recites a sutra, when they return home or to work afterward, they may be told "That's not possible," "It's just an illusion," "It was your imagination," or "You were brainwashed by religion." If their experience was rejected by just two or three people in this way, their conviction could start to waver.

It is said in Buddhism that there are different levels of people's spiritual awareness—the upper, middle, and lower levels. Those having upper-level spiritual awareness will understand the Truth relatively quickly with little teaching, whereas those with middle-level spiritual awareness will require the effort of an average person to reach the same level of enlightenment. Those with lower-level spiritual awareness take time to grasp the Truth despite the many opportunities they have. It is difficult to determine one's own level or guess the level of a particular person. Each level is further divided into three more levels, and everyone's level differs depending on their nature.

The Apostle Paul awakened to his mission Through a mystical experience

Sometimes a highly religious, spiritual person might have lived in a way contrary to the Truth for lack of an opportunity for spiritual awakening but then suddenly does a complete turnaround after a life-changing experience. This is rare, and historically, there have only been a few who have experienced this.

One such example was the conversion of Apostle Paul. Paul had never directly met Jesus while Jesus was alive. Paul was a member of a traditional Jewish church and a priest. He was also officially allowed to arrest the disciples of Jesus, like how the policemen and sheriff could. After the crucifixion of Jesus, he pursued the disciples of Jesus in the area from Jerusalem to present-day Syria, which currently suffers many problems including air strikes. But while he was traveling on the road to Damascus during the day, he suddenly saw a blinding light and fell to the ground. The intense white light blinded him for three days.

Paul, who was at that time called Saul, had his sight restored by Ananias, one of Jesus' disciples. Whereas Jesus had cured a blind man with clay mixed with saliva, Ananias healed Saul by placing his hands on Saul's eyes and praying. Saul experienced the miracle of the restoration of his sight that had been lost due to the white light.

When Saul fell to the ground, he also heard Jesus' voice saying to him, "Saul, Saul, why are you persecuting me?" Saul had in fact been persecuting the disciples of Jesus, but Jesus said "why are you persecuting me?" Until then, Saul had pursued many of the disciples, arrested and executed them, but after his mystical experience, he converted to Christianity.

Once he became a Christian, Paul was accused by both Christians and Jews. The Christians suspected him to be a spy because of his former activities, and the Jews denounced him as a traitor. He was not welcomed by either side and met with a lot of difficulties and hardships. Despite that, he was committed to missionary work throughout his life and died as a martyr like Peter, who was executed on an inverted cross. Such a person existed.

Although Paul formerly had an opposing faith, he had believed in the God of the Jews with a pure heart, so he must have been a religious person. Since Christianity was newly formed and he had never seen Jesus in person, he tried to destroy the new religion and persecuted the disciples of Jesus. He then had a mystical experience and awakened to his true mission. This happens very rarely.

When the light reaches
Into the depth of one's mind

Others have had similar experiences. For example, a person serving a prison sentence suddenly witnessed the presence of Jesus in a mystical experience and became a Christian priest after his release. There was such a case. This kind of conversion does occur, but in general, the person's future is an extension of the person's behavior up to the present and the law of inertia is at work.

Therefore, even if one is brought to a Happy Science shoja and is moved by the holy atmosphere, it is only natural to later have doubts when looking back from a worldly perspective. It would be difficult to overcome such doubt unless one tries to have more friends who share the same faith.

There are also people who have a negative influence on others and start to delude other people. This means their time has yet to come. It is a matter of timing. So, in this case, the only way is to observe them patiently and wait for their time to awaken to the Truth.

Suppose a person works for a company and believes that life is going well—on track for a successful career. Even if he finds Happy Science teachings beneficial and becomes a member, he may not have reached the level of knowing true faith yet. That person may feel deep religious faith only after undergoing some painful experience such as the death of a parent. Some people cannot understand faith until the right time comes.

The other day, as I was listening to our radio program, "Angel's Morning Call," the radio host Ritsuko Shirakura was talking about how she broke into tears after reading the opening message ("A Guide for the Mind") in the Happy Science Monthly Magazine. It was my teaching on the power to forgive sins. I wrote that although people may understand that they should not blame others or the environment for their unhappiness in life and that there is essentially no original sin as believed by Christians, sometimes they might feel like blaming some kind of negative karma to explain their current situation. She said she cried hard after reading that passage.

People with a wide range of experiences may sometimes feel their hearts open up and they directly receive heavenly light. Actress Tomoko Ogawa also experienced this. When she first met me, she apparently felt so much light pouring into her heart that she could not stop crying. I suppose there are others with similar experiences, though not everyone experiences this.

The fact is that everyone has his or her own "time," and you should wait for their time to come. Waiting for their time is also an act of love. Still, it is important to continually provide opportunities for them. This being so, as in the fore-mentioned analogy of pointing at the moon, it is up to the individual whether or not to look at the moon, and it cannot be seen unless the person looks at it with his or her own eyes. Although others can try to show the moon, it is up to the person to look at it in the end.

Know that some people can be saved While others cannot

As you engage in exorcism, you will encounter those who can be saved and those who cannot. It is wrong to assume that failing to save someone means the teachings are wrong or you do not have the ability. Sadly, the ultimate reason for a person not being saved is because he or she lacks virtue. For this reason, you should not be overly shocked. Some people you can save, and some people you cannot. This cannot be helped.

It is certain that everyone—even Happy Science members—will leave this world. Regardless of whether you fall ill or not, everyone will leave this earth with 100 percent certainty. In this sense, it is a bet of "all or nothing" and no other possibilities. However, you can choose how to live your life to make your remaining days fulfilling. Therefore, do not be too simple-minded; be more persistent in your efforts and look at things from a broader perspective. Know that in your life, you can save some people but not all.

Shakyamuni Buddha used the metaphor of a lotus flower to explain the differences in people's spiritual awareness. Lotus flowers bloom in muddy ponds. Some grow up to just below the surface of the water, and with a little help, they can bloom above the waterline. They are like people who will soon awaken to the Truth after listening to some teachings. Some are in the water and need more time to bloom. Yet others are further down near the bottom; they are still budding. It will take much longer for them to reach salvation, and their salvation will not be easy. Shakyamuni Buddha taught that you need to discern more or less at which level others are and then try to present teachings in a way suited to each person. This is the only way.

Jesus Christ performed many miracles, but he said that miracles did not happen in his birthplace. There, many people knew him since his childhood. If the neighbors thought, for example, that he had been naughty, had troubled his mother, had been scolded by his father, or had not been much help as a carpenter, then miracles would have been difficult because faith could not be established. Old friends, relatives, neighbors, and certainly family members knew about his childhood and the time before Jesus attained greatness, so they would not easily believe in him or be his followers.

Now I myself have started building shoja in my hometown, Tokushima Prefecture, but it is possible because many years have passed and I have reached the age of sixty. That is why I am able to build Holy Land El Cantare Seitankan at my birthplace, Kawashima Town. My former friends have mostly reached retirement age. Upon reaching this age, your reputation is mostly set and others would understand the kind of person you are. That is why I felt that it was time to build shoja there. If I had built them in my thirties, I would have probably received more criticism than admiration. At that time, it was better to build shoja in cities where the majority of people did not know about my childhood.

So, it comes down to people, the characteristic of places, and the differences in people's spiritual awareness—the upper, middle, and lower levels. We need to study about human nature as well. Still, ultimately, it is essential to know that it is up to the individual to look at the moon, as taught by Buddha.

AFTERWORD

For those who have had a spiritual experience, it is obvious that humans are the combination of soul and body. What is more, people will experience various demonic temptations as well as receive help from angels at different points in their lives. However, under the guise of science, modern academic study and education have clouded people's eyes to see this simple truth. As a result, the wrong views of atheists, materialists, and of misguided religions have been prevailing.

In general, it is possible to dispel possessing spirits using the CD of my recitation of *The True Words Spoken By Buddha*, my lecture DVDs, the study of Buddha's Truth, and kigan (ritual prayer) at a Happy Science shoja. Even so, the existence of demons and devils cannot be clearly proven in the courts or hospitals.

The exorcism I teach is the most advanced in modern society. It is the integration of what has been taught in fragments in various religions, including Christianity, Islam, Buddhism, and Shintoism. I hope you will learn it thoroughly.

Ryuho Okawa
Master and CEO of Happy Science Group
April 5, 2019

TN: This afterword was given for the Japanese title, *Shin no Exorcist* (compiled as chapters 2-4 of this book).

This book is a compilation of the lectures,
with additions, as listed below.

- Chapter One -
The Modern Exorcist

Japanese title: *Gendai no Exorcist*
Lecture given on June 23, 2001,
at General Headquarters, Happy Science, Tokyo, Japan

- Chapter Two -
Basic Measures to Overcome
Spiritual Disturbance

Japanese title: *Reishou Taisaku no Kihon*
Lecture given on September 5, 2018,
at Special Lecture Hall, Happy Science, Tokyo, Japan

- Chapter Three -
The Real Exorcist

Japanese title: *Shin no Exorcist*
Lecture given on May 9, 2018,
at Special Lecture Hall, Happy Science, Tokyo, Japan

- Chapter Four -
Exorcists as Religious Professionals

Japanese title: *Shukyou no Pro toshiteno Exorcist*
Q&A session given on May 9, 2018,
at Special Lecture Hall, Happy Science, Tokyo, Japan

ABOUT THE AUTHOR

RYUHO OKAWA was born on July 7th 1956, in Tokushima, Japan. After graduating from the University of Tokyo with a law degree, he joined a Tokyo-based trading house. While working at its New York headquarters, he studied international finance at the Graduate Center of the City University of New York. In 1981, he attained Great Enlightenment and became aware that he is El Cantare with a mission to bring salvation to all of humankind. In 1986 he established Happy Science. It now has members in over 100 countries across the world, with more than 700 local branches and temples as well as 10,000 missionary houses around the world. The total number of lectures has exceeded 3,100 (of which more than 150 are in English) and over 2,600 books (of which more than 500 are Spiritual Interview Series) have been published, many of which are translated into 31 languages. Many of the books, including *The Laws of the Sun* have become best sellers or million sellers. To date, Happy Science has produced 20 movies. The original story and original concept were given by the Executive Producer Ryuho Okawa. Recent movie titles are *The Real Exorcist* (live-action movie released in May 2020), *Kiseki to no Deai - Kokoro ni Yorisou 3 -* (lit. "Encounters with Miracles - Heart to Heart 3 -," documentary scheduled to be released in Aug. 2020), and *Twiceborn* (live-action movie to be released in Fall of 2020). He has also composed the lyrics and music of over 100 songs, such as theme songs and featured songs of movies. Moreover, he is the Founder of Happy Science University and Happy Science Academy (Junior and Senior High School), Founder and President of the Happiness Realization Party, Founder and Honorary Headmaster of Happy Science Institute of Government and Management, Founder of IRH Press Co., Ltd., and the Chairperson of New Star Production Co., Ltd. and ARI Production Co., Ltd.

WHAT IS EL CANTARE?

El Cantare means "the Light of the Earth," and is the Supreme God of the Earth who has been guiding humankind since the beginning of Genesis. He is whom Jesus called Father and Muhammad called Allah. Different parts of El Cantare's core consciousness have descended to Earth in the past, once as Alpha and another as Elohim. His branch spirits, such as Shakyamuni Buddha and Hermes, have descended to Earth many times and helped to flourish many civilizations. To unite various religions and to integrate various fields of study in order to build a new civilization on Earth, a part of the core consciousness has descended to Earth as Master Ryuho Okawa.

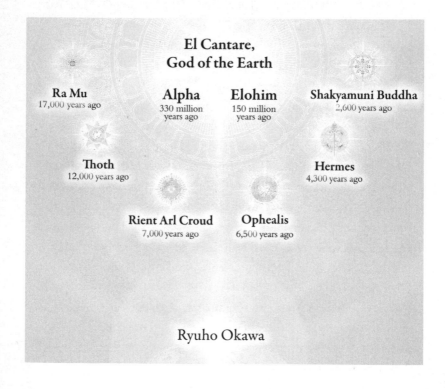

El Cantare,
God of the Earth

Ra Mu
17,000 years ago

Alpha
330 million
years ago

Elohim
150 million
years ago

Shakyamuni Buddha
2,600 years ago

Thoth
12,000 years ago

Hermes
4,300 years ago

Rient Arl Croud
7,000 years ago

Ophealis
6,500 years ago

Ryuho Okawa

Alpha Alpha is a part of the core consciousness of El Cantare that descended to Earth more than 300 million years ago. Alpha preached Earth's Truths to harmonize and unify Earth-born humans and space people who came from other planets.

Elohim Elohim is the name of El Cantare's core consciousness that lived on Earth 150 million years ago. He taught teachings of wisdom, mainly on the differences of light and darkness, good and evil.

Shakyamuni Buddha Gautama Siddhartha was born as a prince into the Shakya Clan in India around 2,600 years ago. When he was 29 years old, he renounced the world and sought enlightenment. He later attained Great Enlightenment and founded Buddhism.

Hermes In the Greek mythology, Hermes is thought of as one of the 12 Olympian gods, but the spiritual Truth is that he taught the teachings of love and progress around 4,300 years ago that became the origin of the current Western civilization. He is a hero that truly existed.

Ophealis Ophealis was born in Greece around 6,500 years ago and was the leader who took an expedition to as far as Egypt. He is the God of miracles, prosperity, and arts, and is known as Osiris in the Egyptian mythology.

Rient Arl Croud Rient Arl Croud was born as a king of the ancient Incan Empire around 7,000 years ago and taught about the mysteries of the mind. In the heavenly world, he is responsible for the interactions that take place between various planets.

Thoth Thoth was an almighty leader who built the golden age of the Atlantic civilization around 12,000 years ago. In the Egyptian mythology, he is known as god Thoth.

Ra Mu Ra Mu was a leader who built the golden age of the civilization of Mu around 17,000 years ago. As a religious leader and a politician, he ruled by uniting religion and politics.

WHAT IS A SPIRITUAL MESSAGE?

We are all spiritual beings living on this earth. The following is the mechanism behind Ryuho Okawa's spiritual messages.

1 You are a spirit

People are born into this world to gain wisdom through various experiences and return to the other world when their lives end. We are all spirits and repeat this cycle in order to refine our souls.

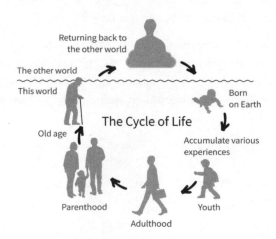

2 You have a guardian spirit

Guardian spirits are those who protect the people living on this earth. Each of us has a guardian spirit that watches over us and guides us from the other world. They are one of our past lives, and are identical in how we think.

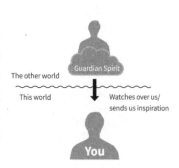

3 How spiritual messages work

Since a guardian spirit thinks at the same subconscious level as the person living on earth, Ryuho Okawa can summon the spirit and find out what the person on earth is actually thinking. If the person has already returned to the other world, the spirit can give messages to the people living on earth through Ryuho Okawa.

1 The guardian spirit / spirit in the other world...

2 Goes inside Ryuho Okawa in this world

3 Okawa speaks the words of the guardian spirit / spirit

The spiritual messages of more than 1,000 sessions have been openly recorded by Ryuho Okawa since 2009, and the majority of these have been published. Spiritual messages from the guardian spirits of living politicians such as U.S. President Trump, Japanese Prime Minister Shinzo Abe and Chinese President Xi Jinping, as well as spiritual messages sent from the Spirit World by Jesus Christ, Muhammad, Thomas Edison, Mother Teresa, Steve Jobs and Nelson Mandela are just a tiny pack of spiritual messages that were published so far.

Domestically, in Japan, these spiritual messages are being read by a wide range of politicians and mass media, and the high-level contents of these books are delivering an impact even more on politics, news and public opinion. In recent years, there have been spiritual messages recorded in English, and English translations are being done on the spiritual messages given in Japanese. These have been published overseas, one after another, and have started to shake the world.

For more about spiritual messages and a complete list of books, visit **okawabooks.com**

ABOUT HAPPY SCIENCE

Happy Science is a global movement that empowers individuals to find purpose and spiritual happiness and to share that happiness with their families, societies, and the world. With more than twelve million members around the world, Happy Science aims to increase awareness of spiritual truths and expand our capacity for love, compassion, and joy so that together we can create the kind of world we all wish to live in.

Activities at Happy Science are based on the Principles of Happiness (Love, Wisdom, Self-Reflection, and Progress). These principles embrace worldwide philosophies and beliefs, transcending boundaries of culture and religions.

> **Love** teaches us to give ourselves freely without expecting anything in return; it encompasses giving, nurturing, and forgiving.

> **Wisdom** leads us to the insights of spiritual truths, and opens us to the true meaning of life and the will of God (the universe, the highest power, Buddha).

> **Self-Reflection** brings a mindful, nonjudgmental lens to our thoughts and actions to help us find our truest selves—the essence of our souls—and deepen our connection to the highest power. It helps us attain a clean and peaceful mind and leads us to the right life path.

Progress emphasizes the positive, dynamic aspects of our spiritual growth—actions we can take to manifest and spread happiness around the world. It's a path that not only expands our soul growth, but also furthers the collective potential of the world we live in.

PROGRAMS AND EVENTS

The doors of Happy Science are open to all. We offer a variety of programs and events, including self-exploration and self-growth programs, spiritual seminars, meditation and contemplation sessions, study groups, and book events.

Our programs are designed to:
* Deepen your understanding of your purpose and meaning in life
* Improve your relationships and increase your capacity to love unconditionally
* Attain peace of mind, decrease anxiety and stress, and feel positive
* Gain deeper insights and a broader perspective on the world
* Learn how to overcome life's challenges
  ... and much more.

*For more information, visit **happy-science.org**.*

INTERNATIONAL SEMINARS

Each year, friends from all over the world join our international seminars, held at our faith centers in Japan. Different programs are offered each year and cover a wide variety of topics, including improving relationships, practicing the Eightfold Path to enlightenment, and loving yourself, to name just a few.

HAPPY SCIENCE MONTHLY

Happy Science regularly publishes various magazines for readers around the world. The Happy Science Monthly, which now spans over 300 issues, contains Master Okawa's latest lectures, words of wisdom, stories of remarkable life-changing experiences, world news, and much more to guide members and their friends to a happier life. This is available in many other languages, including Portuguese, Spanish, French, German, Chinese, and Korean. Happy Science Basics, on the other hand, is a 'theme-based' booklet made in an easy-to-read style for those new to Happy Science, which is also ideal to give to friends and family. You can pick up the latest issues from Happy Science, subscribe to have them delivered (see our contacts page) or view them online.*

* Online editions of the *Happy Science Monthly* and
Happy Science Basics can be viewed at:
info.happy-science.org/category/magazines/

CONTACT INFORMATION

Happy Science is a worldwide organization with faith centers around the globe. For a comprehensive list of centers, visit the worldwide directory at *happy-science.org*. The following are some of the many Happy Science locations:

UNITED STATES AND CANADA

New York
79 Franklin St., New York, NY 10013
Phone: 212-343-7972
Fax: 212-343-7973
Email: ny@happy-science.org
Website: happyscience-na.org

San Francisco
525 Clinton St.
Redwood City, CA 94062
Phone & Fax: 650-363-2777
Email: sf@happy-science.org
Website: happyscience-na.org

New Jersey
725 River Rd, #102B, Edgewater, NJ 07020
Phone: 201-313-0127
Fax: 201-313-0120
Email: nj@happy-science.org
Website: happyscience-na.org

Los Angeles
1590 E. Del Mar Blvd., Pasadena, CA 91106
Phone: 626-395-7775
Fax: 626-395-7776
Email: la@happy-science.org
Website: happyscience-na.org

Florida
5208 8th St., St. Zephyrhills, FL 33542
Phone: 813-715-0000
Fax: 813-715-0010
Email: florida@happy-science.org
Website: happyscience-na.org

Orange County
10231 Slater Ave., #204
Fountain Valley, CA 92708
Phone: 714-745-1140
Email: oc@happy-science.org
Website: happyscience-na.org

Atlanta
1874 Piedmont Ave., NE Suite 360-C
Atlanta, GA 30324
Phone: 404-892-7770
Email: atlanta@happy-science.org
Website: happyscience-na.org

San Diego
7841 Balboa Ave., Suite #202
San Diego, CA 92111
Phone: 619-381-7615
Fax: 626-395-7776
E-mail: sandiego@happy-science.org
Website: happyscience-na.org

Hawaii
Phone: 808-591-9772
Fax: 808-591-9776
Email: hi@happy-science.org
Website: happyscience-na.org

Toronto
845 The Queensway
Etobicoke ON M8Z 1N6 Canada
Phone: 1-416-901-3747
Email: toronto@happy-science.org
Website: happy-science.ca

Kauai
3343 Kanakolu Street, Suite 5
Lihue, HI 96766, U.S.A.
Phone: 808-822-7007
Fax: 808-822-6007
Email: kauai-hi@happy-science.org
Website: kauai.happyscience-na.org

Vancouver
#201-2607 East 49th Avenue
Vancouver, BC, V5S 1J9, Canada
Phone: 1-604-437-7735
Fax: 1-604-437-7764
Email: vancouver@happy-science.org
Website: happy-science.ca

INTERNATIONAL

Tokyo
1-6-7 Togoshi, Shinagawa
Tokyo, 142-0041 Japan
Phone: 81-3-6384-5770
Fax: 81-3-6384-5776
Email: tokyo@happy-science.org
Website: happy-science.org

Seoul
74, Sadang-ro 27-gil,
Dongjak-gu, Seoul, Korea
Phone: 82-2-3478-8777
Fax: 82-2-3478-9777
Email: korea@happy-science.org
Website: happyscience-korea.org

London
3 Margaret St.
London,W1W 8RE United Kingdom
Phone: 44-20-7323-9255
Fax: 44-20-7323-9344
Email: eu@happy-science.org
Website: happyscience-uk.org

Brazil Headquarters
Rua. Domingos de Morais 1154,
Vila Mariana, Sao Paulo SP
CEP 04009-002, Brazil
Phone: 55-11-5088-3800
Fax: 55-11-5088-3806
Email: sp@happy-science.org
Website: happyscience.com.br

Sydney
516 Pacific Hwy, Lane Cove North,
NSW 2066, Australia
Phone: 61-2-9411-2877
Fax: 61-2-9411-2822
Email: sydney@happy-science.org

Jundiai
Rua Congo, 447, Jd. Bonfiglioli
Jundiai-CEP, 13207-340
Phone: 55-11-4587-5952
Email: jundiai@happy-science.org

Taipei

No. 89, Lane 155, Dunhua N. Road
Songshan District, Taipei City 105, Taiwan
Phone: 886-2-2719-9377
Fax: 886-2-2719-5570
Email: taiwan@happy-science.org
Website: happyscience-tw.org

Thailand

19 Soi Sukhumvit 60/1,
Bang Chak, Phra Khanong,
Bangkok, 10260 Thailand
Phone: 66-2-007-1419
Email: bangkok@happy-science.org
Website: happyscience-thai.org

Malaysia

No 22A, Block 2, Jalil Link Jalan Jalil Jaya 2,
Bukit Jalil 57000, Kuala Lumpur, Malaysia
Phone: 60-3-8998-7877
Fax: 60-3-8998-7977
Email: malaysia@happy-science.org
Website: happyscience.org.my

Indonesia

Darmawangsa
Square Lt. 2 No. 225
Jl. Darmawangsa VI & IX
Indonesia
Phone: 021-7278-0756
Email: indonesia@happy-science.org

Nepal

Kathmandu Metropolitan City Ward No. 15,
Ring Road, Kimdol,
Sitapaila Kathmandu, Nepal
Phone: 97-714-272931
Email: nepal@happy-science.org

Philippines Taytay

LGL Bldg, 2nd Floor,
Kadalagaham cor,
Rizal Ave. Taytay,
Rizal, Philippines
Phone: 63-2-5710686
Email: philippines@happy-science.org

Uganda

Plot 877 Rubaga Road, Kampala
P.O. Box 34130, Kampala, Uganda
Phone: 256-79-3238-002
Email: uganda@happy-science.org
Website: happyscience-uganda.org

SOCIAL CONTRIBUTIONS

Happy Science tackles social issues such as suicide and bullying, and launches heartfelt, precise and prompt rescue operations after a major disaster.

◆ The HS Nelson Mandela Fund

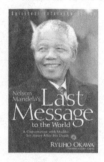

The Happy Science Group provides disaster relief and educational aid overseas via this Fund. We established it following the publication of *Nelson Mandela's Last Message to the World*, a spiritual message from the late Nelson Mandela, in 2013. The fund actively provides both material and spiritual aid to people overseas—support for victims of racial discrimination, poverty, political oppression, natural disasters, and more.

Examples of how the fund has been used:

Provided tents in rural Nepal

Supplied food and water immediately after the Nepal earthquake

Donated a container library to South African primary school, in collaboration with Nelson Mandela Foundation

◆ **We extend a helping hand around the world to aid in post-disaster reconstruction and education.**

NEPAL: After the 2015 Nepal Earthquake, we promptly offered our local temple as a temporary evacuation center and utilized our global network to send water, food and tents. We will keep supporting their recovery via the HS Nelson Mandela Fund.

SRI LANKA: Provided aid in constructing school buildings damaged by the tsunami. Further, with the help of the Sri Lankan prime minister, 100 bookshelves were donated to Buddhist temples.

INDIA: Ongoing aid since 2006—uniforms, school meals, etc. for schools in Bodh Gaya, a sacred ground for Buddhism. Medical aid in Calcutta, in collaboration with local hospitals.

CHINA: Donated money and tents to the Szechuan Earthquake disaster zone. Books were also donated to elementary schools in Gansu Province, near the disaster zone.

UGANDA: Donated educational materials and mosquito nets to protect children from Malaria. Donated a school building and prayer hall to a private secondary school, as well as offering a scholarship to a university student who had graduated from the school.

GHANA: Provided medical supplies as a preventive measure against Ebola.

SOUTH AFRICA: Collaborated with the Nelson Mandela Foundation in South Africa to donate a container library and books to an elementary school.

IRAN: Donated to the earthquake-stricken area in northeastern Iran in October 2012 via the Iranian Embassy.

HAPPINESS REALIZATION PARTY

The Happiness Realization Party (HRP) was founded in May 2009 by Master Ryuho Okawa as part of the Happy Science Group to offer concrete and proactive solutions to the current issues such as military threats from North Korea and China and the long-term economic recession. HRP aims to implement drastic reforms of the Japanese government, thereby bringing peace and prosperity to Japan. To accomplish this, HRP proposes two key policies:

1) Strengthening the national security and the Japan-U.S. alliance, which plays a vital role in the stability of Asia.

2) Improving the Japanese economy by implementing drastic tax cuts, taking monetary easing measures and creating new major industries.

HRP advocates that Japan should offer a model of a religious nation that allows diverse values and beliefs to coexist, and that contributes to global peace.

*For more information, visit **en.hr-party.jp***

HAPPY SCIENCE ACADEMY
JUNIOR AND SENIOR HIGH SCHOOL

Happy Science Academy Junior and Senior High School is a boarding school founded with the goal of educating the future leaders of the world who can have a big vision, persevere, and take on new challenges.

Currently, there are two campuses in Japan; the Nasu Main Campus in Tochigi Prefecture, founded in 2010, and the Kansai Campus in Shiga Prefecture, founded in 2013.

Nasu Main Campus

Kansai Campus

HAPPY SCIENCE UNIVERSITY

THE FOUNDING SPIRIT AND THE GOAL OF EDUCATION

Based on the founding philosophy of the university, "Exploration of happiness and the creation of a new civilization," education, research and studies will be provided to help students acquire deep understanding grounded in religious belief and advanced expertise with the objectives of producing "great talents of virtue" who can contribute in a broad-ranging way to serve Japan and the international society.

FACULTIES

Faculty of Human Happiness

Students in this faculty will pursue liberal arts from various perspectives with a multidisciplinary approach, explore and envision an ideal state of human beings and society.

Faculty of Successful Management

This faculty aims to realize successful management that helps organizations to create value and wealth for society and to contribute to the happiness and the development of management and employees as well as society as a whole.

Faculty of Future Creation

Students in this faculty study subjects such as political science, journalism, performing arts and artistic expression, and explore and present new political and cultural models based on truth, goodness and beauty.

Faculty of Future Industry

This faculty aims to nurture engineers who can resolve various issues facing modern civilization from a technological standpoint and contribute to the creation of new industries of the future.

THE REAL EXORCIST

STORY Tokyo —the most mystical city in the world where you find spiritual spots in the most unexpected places. Sayuri works as a part time waitress at a small coffee shop "Extra" where regular customers enjoy the authentic coffee that the owner brews. Meanwhile, Sayuri uses her supernatural powers to help those who are troubled by spiritual phenomena one after another. Through her special consultations, she touches the hearts of the people and helps them by showing the truths of the invisible world.

BEST FEATURE FILM
17th Angel Film Awards
2020
Monaco International Film Festival

BEST FEMALE ACTOR
17th Angel Film Awards
2020
Monaco International Film Festival

BEST FEMALE SUPPORTING ACTOR
17th Angel Film Awards
2020
Monaco International Film Festival

BEST VISUAL EFFECTS
17th Angel Film Awards
2020
Monaco International Film Festival

BEST FEATURE FILM
EKO International Film Festival
2020

BEST SUPPORTING ACTRESS
EKO International Film Festival
2020

*For more information, visit **www.realexorcistmovie.com***

• Other Happy Science Movies •

1994 **The Terrifying Revelations of Nostradamus**
(live action)

1997 **Love Blows Like the Wind**
(animation)

2000 **The Laws of the Sun**
(animation)

2003 **The Golden Laws**
(animation)

2006 **The Laws of Eternity**
(animation)

2009 **The Rebirth of Buddha**
(animation)

2012 **The Mystical Laws**
(animation)

2015 **The Laws of the Universe - Part 0**
(animation)

2018 **Heart to Heart**
(documentary)

The Laws of the Universe - Part I
(animation)

2019 **The Last White Witch**
(live action)

Life is Beautiful - Heart to Heart 2 -
(documentary)

Immortal Hero
(live action)

2020 **The Real Exorcist**
(live action)

- Coming Soon -

2020 **Kiseki to no Deai - Kokoro ni Yorisou 3 -**
(lit. Encounters with Miracles - Heart to Heart 3 -)
(documentary)

Twiceborn
(live action)

*Contact your nearest local branch for more information on how to watch HS movies.

ABOUT IRH PRESS USA

IRH Press USA Inc. was founded in 2013 as an affiliated firm of IRH Press Co., Ltd. Based in New York, the press publishes books in various categories including spirituality, religion, and self-improvement and publishes books by Ryuho Okawa, the author of over 100 million books sold worldwide. For more information, visit *okawabooks.com*.

Follow us on:

Facebook: Okawa Books **Twitter**: Okawa Books
Goodreads: Ryuho Okawa **Instagram**: OkawaBooks
Pinterest: Okawa Books

RYUHO OKAWA'S LAWS SERIES

The Laws Series is an annual volume of books that are mainly comprised of Ryuho Okawa's lectures on various topics that highlight principles and guidelines for the activities of Happy Science every year. *The Laws of the Sun*, the first publication of the laws series, ranked in the annual best-selling list in Japan in 1987. Since then, all of the laws series' titles have ranked in the annual best-selling list for more than two decades, setting sociocultural trends in Japan and around the world.

THE TRILOGY

The first three volumes of the Laws Series, *The Laws of the Sun*, *The Golden Laws*, and *The Nine Dimensions* make a trilogy that completes the basic framework of the teachings of God's Truths. *The Laws of the Sun* discusses the structure of God's Laws, *The Golden Laws* expounds on the doctrine of time, and *The Nine Dimensions* reveals the nature of space.

BOOKS BY RYUHO OKAWA

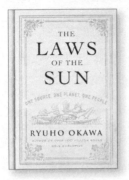

THE LAWS OF THE SUN
ONE SOURCE, ONE PLANET, ONE PEOPLE

Paperback • 288 pages • $15.95
ISBN: 978-1-942125-43-3

Imagine if you could ask God why he created this world and what spiritual laws he used to shape us— and everything around us. In *The Laws of the Sun*, Ryuho Okawa outlines these laws of the universe and provides a road map for living one's life with greater purpose and meaning. This powerful book shows the way to realize true happiness—a happiness that continues from this world through the other.

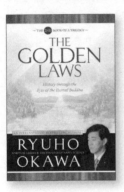

THE GOLDEN LAWS
HISTORY THROUGH THE EYES OF THE ETERNAL BUDDHA

Paperback • 201 pages • $14.95
ISBN: 978-1-941779-81-1

Throughout history, Great Guiding Spirits of Light have been present on Earth in both the East and the West at crucial points in human history to further our spiritual development. *The Golden Laws* reveals how Divine Plan has been unfolding on Earth, and outlines 5,000 years of the secret history of humankind.

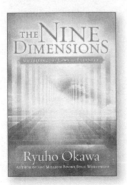

THE NINE DIMENSIONS
UNVEILING THE LAWS OF ETERNITY

Paperback • 168 pages • $15.95
ISBN: 978-0-982698-56-3

This book is a window into the mind of our loving God, who designed this world and the vast, wondrous world of our afterlife as a school with many levels through which our souls learn and grow. When the religions and cultures of the world discover the truth of their common spiritual origin, they will be inspired to accept their differences, come together under faith in God, and build an era of harmony and peaceful progress on Earth.

---

*For a complete list of books, visit **okawabooks.com***

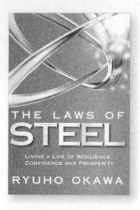

THE LAWS OF STEEL
LIVING A LIFE OF RESILIENCE, CONFIDENCE AND PROSPERITY

Paperback • 256 pages • $16.95
ISBN: 978-1-942125-65-5

This book is a compilation of six lectures that Ryuho Okawa gave in 2018 and 2019, each containing passionate messages for us to open a brighter future. This powerful and inspiring book will not only show us the ways to achieve true happiness and prosperity, but also the ways to solve many global issues we now face. It presents us with wisdom that is based on a spiritual perspective, and a new design for our future society to help us overcome different values and create a peaceful world, thereby ushering in a Golden Age.

THE NEW RESURRECTION
MY MIRACULOUS STORY OF OVERCOMING ILLNESS AND DEATH

Hardcover • 224 pages • $19.95
ISBN: 978-1-942125-64-8

The New Resurrection is an autobiographical account of an astonishing miracle experienced by author Ryuho Okawa in 2004. This event was adapted into the feature-length film *Immortal Hero*, released in Japan, the United States and Canada during the Fall of 2019. Today, Okawa lives each day with the readiness to die for the Truth and has dedicated his life to selflessly guide faith seekers towards spiritual development and happiness. In testament to Okawa's earnest resolve, the appendix showcases a myriad of accomplishments by Okawa, chronicled after his miraculous resurrection.

---

*For a complete list of books, visit **okawabooks.com***

THE HELL YOU NEVER KNEW

AND HOW TO AVOID GOING THERE

Paperback • 192 pages • $15.95
ISBN: 978-1-942125-52-5

From ancient times, people have been warned of the danger of falling to Hell. But does the world of Hell truly exist? If it does, what kind of people would go there? Through his spiritual abilities, Ryuho Okawa found out that Hell is only a small part of the vast Spirit World, yet more than half of the people today go there after they die.

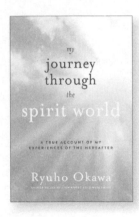

MY JOURNEY THROUGH THE SPIRIT WORLD

A TRUE ACCOUNT OF MY EXPERIENCES OF THE HEREAFTER

Paperback • 224 pages • $15.95
ISBN: 978-1-942125-41-9

What happens when we die? What is the afterworld like? Do heaven and hell really exist? In this book, Ryuho Okawa shares surprising facts such as that we visit the spirit world during sleep, that souls in the spirit world go to a school to learn about how to use their spiritual power, and that people continue to live in the same lifestyle as they did in this world. This unique and authentic guide to the spirit world will awaken us to the truth of life and death, and show us how we should start living so that we can return to a bright world of heaven.

---

*For a complete list of books, visit **okawabooks.com***

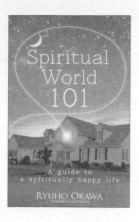

SPIRITUAL WORLD 101
A GUIDE TO A SPIRITUALLY HAPPY LIFE

Paperback • 184 pages • $14.95
ISBN: 978-1-941779-43-9

This book is a spiritual guidebook that will answer all your questions about the spiritual world, with illustrations and diagrams explaining about your guardian spirit and the secrets of God and Buddha. By reading this book, you will be able to understand the true meaning of life and find happiness in everyday life.

THE POSSESSION
KNOW THE GHOST CONDITION AND OVERCOME NEGATIVE SPIRITUAL INFLUENCE

Paperback • 114 pages • $14.95
ISBN: 978-1-943869-66-4

Possession is neither an exceptional occurrence nor unscientific superstition; it's a phenomenon, based on spiritual principles, that is still quite common in the modern society. Through this book, you can find the way to change your own mind and free yourself from possession, and the way to exorcise devils by relying on the power of angels and God.

For a complete list of books, visit **okawabooks.com**

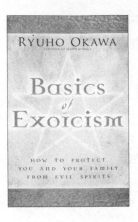

BASICS OF EXORCISM
HOW TO PROTECT YOU AND YOUR FAMILY FROM EVIL SPIRITS

Paperback • 130 pages • $14.95
ISBN: 978-1-941779-34-7

No matter how much time progresses, demons are real. Spiritual screen against curses – the truth of exorcism as told by the author who possesses the six great supernatural powers – The essence of exorcism as a result of more than 5000 rounds of exorcist experience!

UFOS CAUGHT ON CAMERA!
A SPIRITUAL INVESTIGATION ON VIDEOS AND PHOTOS OF THE LUMINOUS OBJECTS VISITING EARTH

Paperback • 112 pages • $17.95
ISBN: 978-1-943869-31-2

In the Summer of 2018, over 60 types of UFOs appeared before the author. UFOs Caught on Camera! is a detailed compilation of Okawa's sightings, with visual analysis of the luminous objects visiting Earth and spiritually sourced commentary of the extraterrestrial intelligence behind them.

For a complete list of books, visit **okawabooks.com**

THE ROYAL ROAD OF LIFE
Beginning Your Path of Inner Peace, Virtue, and a Life of Purpose

THE LAWS OF GREAT ENLIGHTENMENT
Always Walk with Buddha

LOVE FOR THE FUTURE
Building One World of Freedom and Democracy Under God's Truth

THE LAWS OF BRONZE
Love One Another, Become One People

THE LAWS OF INVINCIBLE LEADERSHIP
An Empowering Guide for Continuous and
Lasting Success in Business and in Life

THE STARTING POINT OF HAPPINESS
An Inspiring Guide to Positive Living with Faith, Love, and Courage

HEALING FROM WITHIN
Life-Changing Keys to Calm, Spiritual, and Healthy Living

THE UNHAPPINESS SYNDROME
28 Habits of Unhappy People (and How to Change Them)

THINK BIG!
Be Positive and Be Brave to Achieve Your Dreams

THE MOMENT OF TRUTH
Become a Living Angel Today

---

*For a complete list of books, visit **okawabooks.com***